POSITIVE PARENTING SERIES

Help your child with
The NATIONAL CURRICULUM TESTS

GRAEME KENT

GW00691840

Hodder & Stoughton

A MEMBER OF THE HODDER HEADLINE GROUP

About the author

Graeme Kent has taught in many primary schools at home and overseas. For eighteen years he was the headteacher of St Thomas' Primary School in Boston, Lincs. This was described in the *Independent on Sunday's* selection of Britain's best schools as 'a quite remarkable primary school that seemingly manages to involve everybody – parents, teachers, governors, support staff, local authority councillors – in a drive to get the best for their pupils.' He has written a number of textbooks and books on education, as well as twelve novels. He is the father of two children.

A catalogue record for this title is available from the British Library

ISBN 0 340 70135 8

First published 1997
Impression number   10 9 8 7 6 5 4 3 2 1
Year   2002 2001 2000 1999 1998 1997

Typeset by Wearset, Boldon, Tyne and Wear.
Printed in Great Britain for Hodder & Stoughton Educational, a division of Hodder Headline Plc, 338 Euston Road, London NW1 3BH by Cox & Wyman Ltd, Reading, Berks.

Contents

CHAPTER ONE

Introduction

Helping your child with the National Curriculum tests

Tests

The papers lie there,
Staring at me blankly,
Waiting to be filled.

an adaptation of a haiku, by Jake, aged ten

At different times during your child's school career she will take certain national tests and be graded on them according to the marks she receives. You will be informed of the results of these tests, so that you may see how she compares with other children of the same age.

These tests are important. At different ages they will determine what programmes of education are prepared for your child by her teacher, and which groups of children she will be linked with to receive this teaching. It is fair to say that the type of education your child receives will depend on how she does in the various tests.

There is a great deal that you can do at home to prepare your child for these challenges and make sure that she does herself justice. These activities need little material, should not take up a great deal of time and can be enjoyable as well as useful for you both.

The tests

The tests will be set at four different times in your child's school career. Three of the tests are taken while she is at primary school, and one is taken when she is receiving her secondary education.

Ages at which tests are taken

- Year 1, when children are four or five.
- Year 2, when most children are seven, although a few younger ones may be six.
- Year 6, when most children are eleven, although a few younger ones may be ten.
- Year 9, when most children are fourteen, although a few younger ones may be thirteen.

The subjects

Teachers will be assessing children in all subjects of the National Curriculum throughout their time at school. The results of these assessments will be passed on to you. However, children only take written tests in two subjects in their first and second years at school, and in three subjects in the other two tests.

Subjects tested and assessed

- Year 1:   English, mathematics, social skills (assessed only).
- Year 2:   English, mathematics.
- Year 6:   English, mathematics, science.
- Year 9:   English, mathematics, science.

Grading

Most of these tests will usually be taken at school and marked by the class teacher. Sometimes the marks will be checked by an outside authority. In the case of the Year 9 tests, the papers will be sent away to be marked outside the school. As a result of the marking each child will be graded as below average, average or above average in each subject.

Levels of attainment

Year	Subjects	Scales	Rating
1	English Mathematics Social skills	1 2 3 4	below average below average average above average
2	English Mathematics	1 2 3	below average average above average
6	English Mathematics Science	3 4 5	below average average above average
9	English Mathematics Science	5 6 7 8	average average above average above average

In the tests given in this book the maximum marks obtainable for each subject will give your child a standard equivalent to Level 7. If she does obtain this mark then she is also well on the way to attaining the standard of Level 8.

For a few children it is also possible to achieve an even higher standard in the different subjects. This is known as an *exceptional performance.* If your child falls into this strictly limited category the first inkling you probably will have of it is when the school tries to adopt her!

Standards

There has been a great deal of controversy over the low grad-ings received by many children who have taken the national tests over the last few years. There is absolutely no reason why any child of average ability should do badly in any of the sub-jects. The standards expected are reasonable. Your child will be conscientiously taught at school. All that is missing is the personal touch which you can provide at home and which a teacher busy with a large class cannot provide. By following a few simple exercises at home you can improve your child's potential score considerably, no matter what her age. Thousands of parents have already done this. There is no reason why you cannot be another.

Helping at home

The key word is *familiarity.* The reason why so many children do not achieve high scores in the tests is because they are not familiar with the types of questions they will be asked. When it comes to taking the tests often they panic or freeze. Your child's teacher can provide her with all the necessary skills and knowledge. However, the teacher will not have time to familiarise each child regularly on a one-to-one basis with the sorts of test papers which will be presented.

You can work at home with your child and build on what is being taught at school by preparing her specifically for the questions she will be expected to answer. This is exactly what the teacher would like to do if only she had the twin luxuries of small classes and unlimited time. You have the advantage of being in charge of the smallest possible class – one child. With a ratio of this size you will not even need a great deal of time in which to work at home with your child in order to achieve good results.

When to start preparing your child for the tests

You will not really need to start working with your child until some six months before the date of each test in Years 1, 2 and 6. For Year 9 children it will be better to start preparations about eighteen months before the dates of the tests. Except for the tests undertaken in Year 1 the teacher will have done all the groundwork. All that you have to do is apply the final polish.

If you wish to help your child with the tests in Year 1, start going through the activities suggested in Chapter 2 about eight or nine months before she is due to start school. If the starting date is September, as it often is, then you should start preparations in January. Adjust the starting date accordingly if she is due to start at some other time.

The tests taken in Years 2, 6 and 9 are usually taken in the summer term. If your child is in primary school you should start preparations some time during the summer holiday of the year preceding the start of the year in which the test is to be taken, and carry on when the school year starts. In each case this will give you a year in which to work with your child.

For Year 9 children, who have more ground to cover, you should start helping at home at the beginning of the first term of Year 8. This will give you about a year and a half in which to help your child.

How to work with your child

If you follow the suggestions provided in this book you will need to spend comparatively little time working with your child. The following timetables are suggested.

Test	Subject	Time per week	Total time per week
Year 1	Social skills English Mathematics	20 mins 20 mins 20 mins	60 mins
Year 2	English Mathematics	30 mins 30 mins	60 mins
Year 6 & Year 9	English Mathematics Science	30 mins 30 mins 30 mins	90 mins

If your child wishes to spend more time on her work than this, either in your company or on her own, then by all means let her. Make the time allocation suggested above a regular minimum weekly habit.

Try to allot the same time of day for each session, so that your child becomes accustomed to starting work at the same time each evening or over the weekend.

Using this book

The chapters are divided into the different years in which the tests are taken. Chapter 2 deals with the tests and assessments for Year 1. Chapters 3 and 4 are concerned with the Year 2 tests. Chapters 5, 6 and 7 cover the tests taken in Year 6. Chapters 8, 9 and 10 deal with the Year 9 tests.

Each of these chapters provides you with all the home activities you need to engage in with your child to cover the requirements of the different tests. At the end of each chapter there is a test which your child may take and you can mark, in order to judge the standard she has reached at any given moment.

If your child seems to have done particularly well in a test for one year, let her take the test for the next stage in her school career. The same applies to the activities proposed. You can use this book to draw up your own individual educational programme for your child, fitting its contents to her needs.

Chapter break-downs

Each chapter deals with one of the subjects to be tested each year and is divided into the same sections. A chapter begins with an outline of the tests to be taken, including the number of papers, how many questions are likely to be asked and how much time your child will have to attempt each paper.

The chapter is then sub-divided into the number of sub-sections which have to be covered. For each of these strands there is a section called *what the examiners will be looking for.* This lays out the standards expected of a child reaching one of the grades for the year – below average, average and above average. For each of these grades there are descriptions of *important attainments* which your child should reach to achieve the appropriate grading.

The next section in each chapter is called *studying at home.* This provides details of ways in which you can work with your child to complement the work being done at school and familiarise her with the requirements of the tests. In this section there are a number of *study items,* which give advice on covering important aspects of the timetable which often come up in the test papers. There are also lists of *key facts* which your child should memorise.

Each chapter ends with an appropriate test which you can give your child, together with the answers. Time limits are suggested. Some of the questions in these tests are set out in the same way as those in the real tests. A number, however, are set out in other ways. This is to make sure that your child really understands the topic being covered and will have the confidence to tackle it, no matter how the questions may be couched. Some of the questions have been broken down into their component parts in order to make it easier for you to mark your child's work.

Parents talking

❛ My husband, who is a police sergeant, got very keen on helping our child at home with her tests, so he went in his civilian clothes to a special parents' evening in the school to discuss this. Unfortunately that evening a crazed bullock got loose from the local abattoir and reached the school. It ran snorting round and round the outside of the hall for about half an hour, smashing up cars, while the teachers and parents cowered inside. My husband was in a particularly petrified state in case someone remembered that he was a policeman and demanded that he went out and dealt with the animal. In the end the abattoir staff arrived and led the bullock away. Somehow my husband lost all interest in liaison with the school after that. He said he felt safer out on the streets dealing with criminals. ❜

Useful books for parents

Bringing School Home, Ruth Merttens and Jeff Vass, Hodder and Stoughton.
Key Stage 1 of the National Curriculum, Ted Wragg, Longman.
Key Stage 2 of the National Curriculum, Ted Wragg, Longman.
Key Stage 3 of the National Curriculum, Ted Wragg, Longman.
Help your child with homework and exams, Jennie Lindon, Positive Parenting series, Headway, Hodder and Stoughton.

CHAPTER TWO

Tests and assessments for four- and five-year-olds

Quiet
(a message to new children at the school)

It
is nice.
God tells us
to be quiet.
You cannot see it.
Our head says it
all the time
to us
all.

Lynne, aged ten

In your child's first term at school he will be tested over a number of areas, to see what he is capable of. He will receive a written test in reading, writing and arithmetic, which should last about 20 minutes. He will also be assessed by his teacher on what are termed 'social skills'.

In each of these tests and assessments your child will be rated on an ability scale of 1 to 4. Scales 1 and 2 will denote that your child is generally regarded as below average for his age in the area being tested. Scale 3 should be reached by the average four- or five-year-old boy or girl. A rating of Scale 4 will mean that your child is well above average.

The standards expected of a child starting school are not exacting and there is no reason why your child should not do well in the tests and assessments, especially if you give him a little help at home. When the government's official advisory body, the Schools Curriculum and Assessment Authority, published the results of its pilot study into these tests in 1996 – which was carried out among thousands of children – it announced that there were two types of children who scored particularly well. The first of these groups were boys and girls who had been to nursery school. The second section scoring high consistently were those children who had received good family support.

Social skills

In your child's first weeks at school, as he goes about his everyday activities in and out of the classroom, he will be observed closely by his teacher in order for her to give him a rating for his social skills, or ability to cope with school, and the children and adults he encounters there. Specifically he will be graded on a number of skills.

What the teacher will be looking for

In any child starting school the teacher will hope to find a sensible, confident, well-adjusted child with a firm grasp of certain basic skills and abilities, the ability to fit in to a new environment and a willingness to try new things on his own.

Study item: basic skills looked for

- Ability to cope with elementary skills.
- Ability to mix with others.
- Independence and confidence.
- Willingness to try new things.

TESTS AND ASSESSMENTS FOR FOUR- AND FIVE-YEAR-OLDS

Studying elementary skills at home

Most of the skills your child should possess when he starts school are a matter of common sense. He will be in a class of up to thirty other children and if he needs individual attention with every basic function he will feel different and will lose self-esteem, which will have an effect upon his school work. Before he starts school there are a number of ways in which you can help him to embark upon his life there with confidence and enable him to get the best from the school.

Help him to take an interest in the world around him, examining and recognising shapes and colours. Show him that materials may have different textures which he can feel and describe. Assist him to cope with his world, which is growing larger every day.

Study item: using the lavatory
Make sure that your child can:

- go to the lavatory on his own
- operate toilet rolls
- use different types of flush
- wash his hands afterwards.

It might be that the type of flush used in the school toilets is different from the ones you have at home. See if you can find out which sort are in operation at school. If they are different, find a replica somewhere of the school's type, in order to give him practice in using it.

Study item: making wants known
Help your child to:

- speak clearly
- ask for what he wants succinctly and politely
- know when to say 'please' and 'thank you'
- wait for a suitable moment to speak.

Study item: dressing and undressing

Teach your child to:

- operate any buttons or zips on clothing
- tie and untie shoelaces
- generally be able to dress and undress unaided.

If your child has trouble with shoelaces, there are plenty of shoes available with velcro fastenings. If there is no specified school uniform, check in advance what the other children in the class wear. It will be a source of great mortification, for example, if your son is the only boy in the class not wearing long trousers!

It will also be a help if you make sure that your child knows his name and address and can repeat them if asked. He will also be judged on his ability to cope as a member of the class. He should be helped in advance to become accustomed to answering questions. Spend some time with him, asking simple questions like 'Where have you been?', 'Are you cold?', and so on. Encourage him to answer fully, in complete sentences, not in single words.

Ensure that your child understands the use of everyday objects. School can be a daunting place at first, and the slightest thing can prove a setback to his confidence. He will want to fit in from the first and show that he can do everything that the others can.

Study item: using everyday objects

Help your child to use:

- door-knobs and latches
- doors which swing both ways
- taps
- cutlery.

Help your child to get used to other children and learn how to get on with them. If he can gain experience at a play-group or nursery school this will help. If there are no facilities for these locally, then try to join with other parents of young children once or twice a week to let the children get together under supervision. Make sure that your child uses these meetings to learn to share and take turns. In those important first days at school the teacher will be looking for signs that he can talk to individuals and to groups without fear, and that he can also listen attentively to both adults and other children.

It will benefit your child if you prepare him for the initial leaving of home to start school by starting to leave him with friends or relations for a few hours at a time, so that on the first day of school the sudden departure of the parent does not upset him. He will know by then that you always come back.

Reading

There are wide disparities between the reading skills of different children when they start school at four or five. Some will have no abilities in this direction at all, while others already will be accustomed to handling books and recognising letters, words and sentences. Your child will be graded according to his basic reading skills in his first few weeks at school.

What the teacher will be looking for

At the very least the teacher will hope that your child can recognise his own name when it is written down. If he can recognise the initial sounds of words – *a*, *b*, and so on – this will also help. To be graded as an average reader for a four- or five-year-old, the teacher will want him to recognise all the letters of the alphabet by their sounds and their shapes.

Studying reading at home

If your child takes to reading even before he starts school it will enhance his progress in all aspects of the school curriculum. Allow him to see you reading for pleasure at home. If he sees you reading newspapers, magazines and books then he may want to do so as well.

Read to your child regularly every day. Choose well-illustrated, short books at first. Make him a part of this reading experience by cuddling him, showing him the pictures in the book and talking about them as you read the story.

After a while he should develop a liking for certain books and ask you to read them to him again. This is a good sign, showing that he is beginning to discriminate and make decisions.

You may even find that he has memorised certain favourite passages from the books and will say them aloud as you read. This means that he is developing his memory.

Gradually extend the range of books you read together. Introduce him to the letters of the alphabet by using one of the many alphabet books on the market, the heavily illustrated sort saying 'a is for apple', and so on.

Prepare for the time when your child will start reading himself by introducing him to the mechanics of reading and using books.

Study item: handling books

- Handle books carefully, with the title the right way up on the cover and on the front page.
- Always handle books with care and respect.
- Read the left-hand page first and then go on to the right-hand page.
- Then turn over and go through the same process again.
- Start to read at the top of a page and go down to the bottom of the page.
- Start to read a line on the left-hand side and proceed to the right-hand side.
- Play games together until you are sure that your child knows the meanings of *top, bottom, left, right.*

The next stage will be to introduce your child to the letters of the alphabet. The best way to do this is to follow up the alphabet book you are reading together by buying a set of the 26 letters in plastic. Purchase the lower-case letters first. Most toy shops will stock them.

Show him the letters, one at a time, and talk about them. Encourage him to handle the letters. After a time he should begin to recognise some of them by associating them with shapes – 'o is round', 's is like a snake'.

If he enjoys doing this, start testing him to see which letters he recognises. Use your alphabet book and show your child the picture only, not the letter. See if he can say that the picture of an apple begins with the letter *a*, and can show you from the pile of letters before him what this letter looks like.

If your child seems ready for it, let him read his own very simple books. These should be picture-books with an abundance of illustrations and comparatively little text. There are some excellent books for pre-school readers by Janet and Allan Ahlberg, published by Heinemann, while for an older generation the *Thomas the Tank Engine and Friends Easy-to-Read* series, by the Rev. W. Awdry and Ken Stott, published by Mammoth, are also very good. A more detailed booklist may be found at the end of this chapter.

Writing

Obviously, the better your child can read the better he will be able to write. Some children arrive at school with a firm grasp of the basics of writing, while others can hardly hold a pencil.

What the teacher will be looking for

Your child's teacher will hope that at the very least he will be able to put something down on paper and tell her from these efforts which is supposed to be print and which are pictures. A slightly more advanced child will be expected to have a go at writing at least a few letter-type shapes. The average child ought to be able to write his own name correctly. A child of above average ability at this stage would be able to write whole words.

Studying writing at home

If your child is making good progress at reading and is able to distinguish between different letters, even if only to a limited degree, encourage him to start writing.

At first this will consist only of showing him how to hold a thick pencil and letting him scribble on thick sheets of paper. From this you can go on to encourage him to try his hands at simple pictures, drawing pin-men, and so on.

If your child makes good progress in this direction, which means that he should be handling a pencil easily and knows most of the letters of the alphabet, you can start to show him how to start learning the preliminary stages of forming letters.

Study item: approach to forming letters

- Practise drawing straight lines – horizontal and vertical.
- Practise drawing circles.
- Form letters using vertical lines or half-lines – *i, l.*
- Put some horizontal and vertical lines together to form letters – *t.*
- Put some vertical lines and circles together to form letters – *b, d, g, q.*

If your child shows enthusiasm for and ability at forming letters in this manner, go on to show him how to form letters properly. Letters are formed by drawing lines, loops, circles and semi-circles in different ways and joining them.

Study item: forming letters

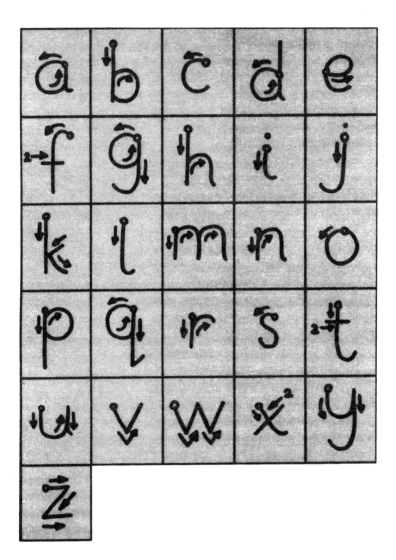

Very few pre-school children will learn how to form all the letters of the alphabet, but if yours is one of them let him go on to learn how to write his own name. For this exercise teach him the necessary upper case letters for the first letters of his Christian name and surname. As an extra bonus, you could also encourage him to write a few short words, e.g. *hat, dog,* etc. At this stage he should be using unjoined letters only.

Speaking and listening

Your child's teacher will also want to see how well he can speak and listen, as these skills form two important parts of the National Curriculum throughout the primary school.

What the teacher will be looking for

A child with only a limited grasp of speaking skills should still be able to talk about things he has seen or experienced. A child with a slightly better grasp of oral language should be able to ask questions in order to find things out, and listen to the answers. A child of average ability ought to be capable of making up a story and telling it. A few children, those of above average ability for this age, should be able to tell a story with a number of details to a small group, and listen to the stories of others.

Studying speaking and listening at home

Spend five minutes every day, preferably out of doors, just listening with your child. This will help heighten his powers of perception. When the five minutes are over, ask him what he has heard during the listening period. Help him to remember – the song of birds, the sound of a lawnmower, etc. Practice of this sort will help him to concentrate.

Few pre-school children need to be encouraged to talk, but you can direct the way in which your child uses language. Encourage him to ask questions. This will help him to sort out his ideas, develop his vocabulary and begin to listen, so by listening to the answers he can learn.

Encourage him to talk about the stories you are reading together and to tell you what he thinks about them. Discuss the characters in the stories and see if your child can make up further adventures for them.

The teacher will also be looking out for signs that he has some knowledge and understanding of his immediate world. Talk to him about members of the family, trying to make him understand that some things happened in the past while others are occurring now. Discuss and show him the area in which you live, and tell him the names of such basic aspects of the environment as roads, shops, hills and rivers.

Mathematics

If you can spend half an hour a week introducing your child to the basics of mathematics, this will help him greatly when he starts school and takes the first tests.

What the teacher will be looking for

The teacher will hope that at least your child will be able to recite the numbers 1 to 5. If he is slightly more advanced he will be able to sort items into groups – five counters in one pile, another five counters in another pile, and so on. A child of average ability at this age should be able to recognise numbers up to 10 and be able to write 1 to 10. A child of above average ability will also be able to count backwards from 10 to 1.

Studying mathematics at home

There are a number of ways in which your child can be prepared for the tests he will take at the age of four or five. These activities will help him understand the basic concepts or ideas of mathematics. While you are working with your child make sure that you use the vocabulary of mathematics, so that he becomes accustomed to hearing such words as big, small, take, add, etc.

Study item: mathematics tasks at home

- Look for patterns. How are things the same?
- Put objects into groups by size (big, small, etc), shape (round, flat, etc) colour, and so on.
- Look for order. Put objects in order of size (big, bigger, biggest, tall, taller, tallest, etc).
- Match items. From a pile of objects take out two blocks of the same size and colour, two matches, etc.
- Learn *ordinal* position. This means putting objects in order – first, second, third, etc. A child of above average ability will start school being able to do this up to tenth place.
- Be able to add objects together.
- Be able to take objects away from a group and count (a) the number taken away, and (b) the number left.

There are many games which you can make up and play with your child which will involve these aspects of mathematics. While you are playing these games make sure that you keep mentioning the numbers involved. 'We shall put *two* blocks here, and *three* blocks there.' Play games with counters in which you ask your child to count out a certain number from a pile. Start with one counter and two counters and gradually work your way up to ten.

When you are sure that he understands the idea of numbers meaning the same as amounts, start showing him the figures which represent the different numbers up to ten. Draw each of these numbers on a separate piece of cardboard and show each one in turn to him, asking him to tell you which amount the number represents. As he tells you the number ask him to take that amount of counters from a pile.

He will stumble and make mistakes at first, but if you both persevere it should not take long at all for him to learn the numbers and what they represent.

ASSESSMENT AND TESTS – FIRST TERM

You should take a full part in these tests and assessments with your child. For the personal and social development assessments be as objective as possible, observing your child over a period of time and ticking each box as appropriate.

With the English and mathematics tests go through the papers with your child, reading out the questions and then sitting back to let him work out the answers.

Do not spend much more than 20 minutes each on the English and the mathematics tests.

Personal and social development assessment

The child can

1 speak clearly ☐
2 ask for what he wants ☐
3 use 'please' and 'thank you' appropriately ☐
4 mix with other children easily ☐
5 dress and undress himself ☐
6 tie and untie shoelaces ☐
7 handle door-knobs, taps and latches ☐
8 use a knife and fork ☐
9 use the toilet and wash his hands afterwards ☐
10 clear up toys and possessions after use ☐
11 share possessions with others ☐
12 work on his own for a limited period ☐
13 work on his own for quite long periods ☐
14 respond to suggestions from adults ☐
15 treat possessions with care ☐
16 treat pets with care ☐
17 work in a group ☐
18 be sensitive to the needs of others ☐
19 handle unfamiliar people and situations confidently ☐
20 lead a group ☐

HELP YOUR CHILD WITH THE NATIONAL CURRICULUM TESTS

English – Reading

1 Which of these is the right way up for the front cover of a book?

(a)   (b)   (c)

2 Look at these letters and pictures. Which one is the letter?

(a)   (b)   (c)

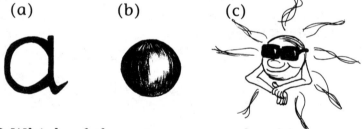

3 Which of these two pages should you read first? (a) left page (b) right page

4 Where should you start reading this page?

Once upon a time there was a jungle. Richie was one of the tigers living in this jungle.

Every day he woke up bright and early - ready for an adventure.

- 1 -

(a) in the middle
(b) on the top right-hand side
(c) on the bottom at the left?

5 Where should you start reading this line?

Once upon a time there was a party.

(a) at the left-hand side
(b) in the middle
(c) on the right-hand side

6 Write down the first five letters of the alphabet.

English – Writing

7 Write down your name.

What are these objects? Write your answer under each one.

8   **9**   **10**

11 Put a full stop in the right place in this sentence.

The boy ran away

English – Speaking and Listening

Listen while this poem is read to you. Then speak clearly and answer the questions on it.

Jack and Jill

Jack and Jill
Went up the hill
To fetch a pail of water.
Jack fell down, and broke his crown,
And Jill came tumbling after.

12 Who were the children in the poem?

13 Where did they go?

14 Why did they go there?

15 What happened to Jack?

16 What happened to Jill?

17 What do you think the word 'tumbling' means?

18 What do you like about this poem?

19/ Draw a picture showing what
20 happened in the poem

Mathematics

Write down how many counters there are in each of these piles.

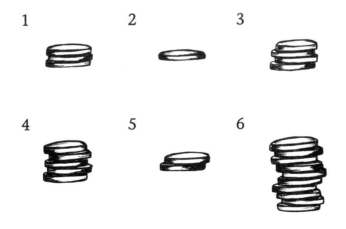

1   2   3

4   5   6

7   8   9

10

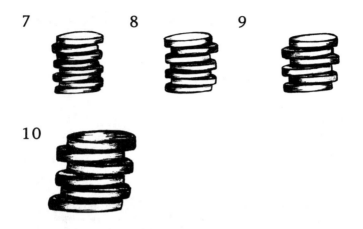

11 What will come next in this pattern?

12 Put a 1 under the biggest box.

(a)   (b)   (c)

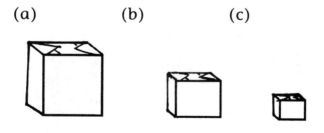

TESTS AND ASSESSMENTS FOR FOUR- AND FIVE-YEAR-OLDS

13 Put a 1 under the biggest mouse.

(a) (b) (c)

14 Draw a line under the two animals which are the same.

15 Draw a line under the two shapes which are the same.

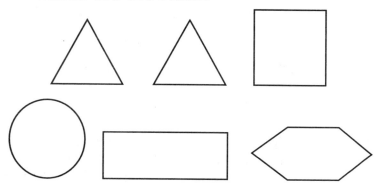

16 Bill, Mary and John run a race. Mary is the winner. John comes next. Bill comes after John. What words do we use to say where they came in the race?

Mary was f...............
Bill was   s ....
John was   th............

Take three counters from each of the following piles. How many counters are left in each pile afterwards?

17   **18**

19  **20**

Test answers

Reading

1 b
2 a
3 a
4 b
5 a
6 a b c d e

Writing

7 Name of child
8 Cat
9 Dog
10 Book
11 Full stop after *away* at end of sentence.

Speaking and listening

12 Jack and Jill
13 Up the hill
14 To fetch a pail of water
15 He fell down
16 She came tumbling after (or she fell down as well)
17 Falling or rolling

18 Give a mark for any sensible answer.

19–20 Give two marks for any drawing showing a scene from the poem.

Mathematics

1	3	**11**	A square
2	1	**12**	a
3	4	**13**	b
4	5	**14**	Two cats
5	2	**15**	Two triangles
6	10	**16**	First, second, third
7	8	**17**	3
8	9	**18**	1
9	7	**19**	7
10	6	**20**	4

Gradings

Give one mark for each tick in the personal and social assessment column and one mark for each correct answer in the English and mathematics tests.

Ratings for Personal and social development assessment, English and mathematics

Marks	Scale	Rating
14–20	1	above average
8–13	2	average
5–8	3	below average
0–5	4	below average

Overall ratings

Marks	Scale	Rating
41–60	1	above average
24–40	2	average
15–23	3	below average
0–14	4	below average

Parents talking

❝ I feel so inadequate trying to set standards for my child. It's not me at all. I feel as if I'm breaking in a new personality for a friend. ❞

❝ One of the strangest experiences I've ever had is seeing my young child learn the names of things. Those things always seemed so much more real to her once she knew what they were called. Perhaps that's how teachers get a kick out of their job. ❞

Useful books for Year 1 tests and assessment

Parents
Entertaining and Educating Your Pre-school Child, Robin Gee and Susan Meredith, Usborne.
Prepare your child for school, Clare Shaw, Positive Parenting series, Headway, Hodder and Stoughton.

Children
Starting school, Janet and Allan Ahlberg, Picture Puffin.
The Oxford Nursery Book, Ian Beck, O.U.P.
The Animals of Farthing Wood series, Colin Dann, Red Fox.
Sing a song of sixpence, Vince Cross, O.U.P.
Spot series, Eric Hill, Picture Puffin.

CHAPTER THREE

English tests for six- and seven-year-olds

Ghost Story

‘ *Mr and Mrs Smith made some new friends called Mr and Mrs Brown. Mr and Mrs Brown asked Mr and Mrs Smith to come to tea the next week. The next week Mr and Mrs Smith came to tea with Mr and Mrs Brown. Mr and Mrs Brown seemed scared. Then Mrs Smith said, "I've just remembered. I've made a mistake with the date. We should have come to tea yesterday, not today." Mrs Brown said, "Yes you should have, and you did!"* ’

Caroline, aged seven

When your child is in Year 2, usually at the age of seven, she will be tested to see what standards of reading, writing and spelling she has attained. There will be two reading tests, one writing test and a spelling test. The tests are not timed but none should occupy more than 45 minutes.

As a result of these tests your child will be given an overall grading in English at Key Stage 1.

ENGLISH TESTS FOR SIX- AND SEVEN-YEAR-OLDS

Reading

By the time she takes the Key Stage 1 tests your child should be able to read silently to herself and show that she understands what she has read, by answering questions on the contents of the reading matter.

She will be expected to read and respond to stories, poems and simple non-fiction texts, like instructions. In the tests she will probably be given two booklets, each containing a different piece of reading matter. The first one will be easier than the second. The teacher will go through several sample questions at the beginning of each book, just to familiarise your child with what she is expected to do. Your child will then be given a certain amount of time to read through each story and poem and then will be expected to answer questions about the stories.

Stories

The stories will be short and interesting and your child should enjoy reading them. She will be asked questions about the story provided with the test paper and the teacher will also assess her reading ability by listening to her reading from a book selected by the teacher.

What the examiners will be looking for

At this stage, when children have only had two or three years at school, the examiners will mainly want to be sure that your child has mastered the basic skills of reading and can understand and appreciate what she has read. The standards laid down are not particularly demanding and a child who is helped at home should be able to cope quite easily with the test papers.

A child of below average ability will be graded at Level 1 and will be expected to understand simple words. An average child will be graded at Level 2 and should be able to read simple texts quite fluently. To attain the above average grading of Level 3 a child ought to be able to read and understand an increasing variety of texts.

Helping with reading tests at home

The better your child can read, the higher the score she will receive in the tests. It is as simple as that. At school the teacher will be taking every opportunity to help your child with her reading skills. There are many simple and useful one-to-one activities, that you can enjoy with your child at home which will make her a better reader and well able to approach the Key Stage 1 tests with confidence.

Besides encouraging her to read as much as possible and to talk about what she has read, it is important to help her to be able to pick out the main points of each story. The stories provided in the Key Stage 1 tests are not long ones and it should be possible for your child to pick out the salient points with ease, especially if you help her regularly with a few basic exercises. The following activities could be applied to each story your child reads at home, preferably not too long after she has finished it, and before she starts the next one. The books she should be reading at this age will not be long ones. If she can read at least one book a week and undertake these activities with you, her approach to books and reading should develop rapidly.

Make these activities low-key and pleasurable for you both. Most children of this age enjoy contact with their parents and displaying newly acquired skills and knowledge. Start by going through the following outline with your child in order to make sure that she has understood what she has read. You can talk about the book under these headings. Do not ask your child to write down anything for herself until you have been doing this for about a year. The contact between you and the interest you are obviously showing in her are very important at this point. The fact that you are also helping her prepare for the tests is just a bonus.

Study item: analysing a book

- The book I have just read is called _____.
- The people in it are _____.
- The story is about _____.
- The story begins _____.
- The story ends _____.
- The bit in it I like best is _____.

It is important, of course, that you have read the book yourself, at first perhaps with your child and then, when she prefers to read alone, separately. After your child has discussed the different aspects of the book, but not before, tell her what you think of the story and discuss the events and characters with her.

The stories in the tests will usually be illustrated. For the less confident reader this will sometimes prove a help, especially if the story is about, say, a less familiar animal, like a badger or a weasel. Encourage your child to take note of the illustrations in the books she reads at home and to relate them to the stories. After you have discussed the story together go back and look at the illustrations and talk about them on the following lines:

Study item: analysing information

- What is each picture about?
- Does it show you one of the people or animals from the story?
- Does the person or animal look like you imagined it to be?
- If not, how is it different?
- Do any of the pictures show you a part of the story?
- Is this part of the story important?
- Why do you think it is important?

Give your child opportunities to rewrite some of the shorter stories in her own words, providing her own illustrations.

If your child is to reach Level 3, the above average standard, she will need to have a firm knowledge of the alphabet and know how to place words in alphabetical order. Go through the alphabet with her and make sure that she can say the alphabet and write it down correctly. About once a week give her a test in placing simple words in alphabetical order. Select half a dozen words from a dictionary, mix them up and ask your child to write them down in the right order.

Study item: alphabetical order

- Write down these words in alphabetical order, according to the first letter of each word:

  horse bat dog sailor cash umbrella

Each week write down the alphabet but leave a few letters out, putting dots in their places. Leave out different letters each week. Ask your child to write in the missing letters.

Study item: missing letters

- Write in the missing letters of the alphabet in the line below:

  a b _ d e _ g h i _ k l _ n _ p q _ s _ u
  _ w x _ z

At this stage your child will also be expected to understand other kinds of writing besides stories. She may be asked in the tests to show that she has understood written instructions by responding to them correctly. Let your child see you reading instructions, recipes, etc, and responding to them, so that she accepts their importance and usefulness. Then let her look at simple written instructions and see if she can follow them.

Study item: instructions

- Read how to use simple tools and kitchen implements.
- Follow simple recipes.
- Follow the Green Cross Code and other safety manuals.
- Memorise the sequence of traffic lights.
- Respond to invitations.

- Learn simple dance steps.
- Learn basic gymnastic movements and sequences.
- Follow instructions as to how to play board games.

Writing

Your child will also be asked to write a simple story. Her handwriting will be assessed as a part of the finished story. She may be asked to write a story of her own choice or be given help in selecting a subject.

What the examiners will be looking for

The examiners will expect your child to be able to write an interesting and well-constructed story in legible handwriting.

As usual, a rating of Level 1 will represent a below average standard. A child at this level will be expected to use simple words and phrases. Level 2 will represent the average expected for this age-group and a child achieving it should be able to write simple stories. Level 3 will be an above average rating at which a child can use sentences in order to write stories, instructions, etc, showing some awareness of basic grammar.

Studying writing at home

If you can help your child to write simple, interesting stories and use other forms of writing, with some use of full stops and a sensible choice of words, then she should reach a Level 2 standard with little difficulty. However, with the sort of one-to-one assistance a parent can provide at home it should be quite possible to help your child reach Level 3 in the Writing test.

At this age there are two main writing skills which are important for your child to master and with which you can help her at home. The first is showing her how to put together or construct a simple story. The second is helping her to produce different forms of writing for different audiences.

Constructing a story

When you discuss the stories your child has read or is reading, keep pointing out that a story has a beginning, a middle and an end. Talk about these parts of the story, until it becomes second nature for your child to divide stories up in this manner. It will not detract from her liking for reading and it will give you an opportunity to share experiences with her. When the time comes to take the tests, this knowledge should inform her own writing and make it structured and interesting, two factors which the examiners will be looking for.

First, help your child to discover that the beginning of a story should involve the reader and make her want to read on.

Study item: beginnings of stories

Story	Beginning
Ali Baba and the 40 Thieves	Ali Baba, a poor wood-cutter, is working in a forest when he sees a group of robbers roll back the mouth of a cave by uttering the magic words, 'Open Sesame!'
Jack and the Beanstalk	Jack and his mother fall upon hard times. Jack takes their cow to market to sell it, but instead swaps it for some magic beans.
Snow White and the Seven Dwarfs	Snow White's step-mother becomes jealous of her and hires a huntsman to take the girl out into a forest and kill her.

As you read stories with your child, make a point of discussing the openings. See how each writer tries to involve the reader from the beginning. How is the main character in the story introduced to the reader? Encourage your child to write her own openings for stories.

Study item: openings of stories

- Try to introduce the main character in the first sentences.
- Make something interesting or unusual happen to this character, which makes it set out on an adventure or an unusual set of events.

After a time start to discuss with your child how the different stories develop from their beginnings. In most stories, what has happened at the beginning launches the main character or characters into a series of steps which make up the main story – the middle of the tale.

Study item: development of stories

Story	Middle
Ali Baba and the 40 Thieves	Ali Baba uses the password he has heard and enters the cave. It is full of gold and jewels. He takes some and becomes rich, but the robbers discover what he has done and set out to find and punish him.
Jack and the Beanstalk	Jack plants the magic beans. A great beanstalk grows, towering up to the sky. Jack climbs it and finds himself in the kingdom of a dreadful giant. Jack finds a hen which lays golden eggs, but he is captured by the giant.
Snow White and the Seven Dwarfs	The huntsman is too kind to kill Snow White and releases her. She is looked after by seven dwarfs. Her step-mother finds her and poisons her, causing her to fall unconscious.

As you discuss the middles of stories you and your child are reading together, point out that these are the longest parts of the stories. The middle is the main part of the tale. It leads on from something which has happened at the beginning – Jack obtaining the magic beans, Ali Baba discovering the password, Snow White being banished from her home, etc.

Talk to your child about the middle of each story and see if you can get her to tell you how this central part of the tale usually ends. See if she can work out that at this stage the main character is in some sort of trouble. Snow White has fallen unconscious. Ali Baba is being hunted by the 40 thieves. Jack is a prisoner of the giant.

Study item: middle of stories

- Make this the longest part of your story.
- Something unusual or interesting happens as a result of the beginning of the story.
- At the end of this part of the story, the main character will often be in some sort of trouble or difficulty.

When your child seems comfortable with the way in which most stories seem to develop from beginnings to middles, starting looking at the endings of the stories you are reading together. In most of them the main character will get out of the trouble he is in and either return to his normal life or go on to a better one.

Study item: endings of stories

Story	Ending
Ali Baba and the 40 Thieves	Ali Baba outwits the 40 thieves, persuading them to hide in large oil jars from which they cannot escape, leaving Ali Baba to enjoy his wealth.
Jack and the Beanstalk	Jack plays upon a magic harp and lulls the giant to sleep, enabling him to escape with the hen which laid the golden eggs.

Snow White and the Seven Dwarfs	A handsome young prince, lost in the forest, finds Snow White. He has the power to arouse her from her stupor. They fall in love and marry.

On a regular basis, study the endings of the stories you read with your child. See how many of them end with the main character getting out of trouble and going on to a better life.

Study item: concluding stories

- The main character uses his intelligence or receives help from someone or something, and gets out of trouble.
- The main character goes back to his old life or on to a better one.

Non-narrative writing

Stories are known as narrative writing because they have plots and characters and tell tales. Your child may also be asked to show that she has a firm grasp of language by being asked to produce an example of non-narrative writing, or to answer questions about such a piece. If you can get your child to read and write across a wide range of materials this will supplement the work she is doing at school.

Let your child see in everyday use in the home examples of such forms of writing as diaries, invitations, lists, recipes, poems, messages, instructions, notes. When she has grown accustomed to seeing you using and referring to these, give her the opportunity to try her hand at producing her own. The simplest form of writing to start with is a list. Make sure that your child gets accustomed to taking care that she makes her lists comprehensive, so that they are really helpful.

Study item: lists

Make lists of:
- jobs to do in the house

- things to take to school
- items to buy from a shop
- articles to take on a journey
- words to learn to spell
- books to get from a library.

Another simple form of writing is the recipe. Show your child how to cook something simple and then ask her to write down the recipe you have just given her, so that you can cook the object together. Check that the recipe she has prepared is accurate. Make this a regular weekly or monthly occurrence.

Get into the habit of leaving your child simple notes and written messages, asking her to do things, and see if she can understand what is wanted of her. In return ask her to make and give you her own notes.

If you are going to have a children's party, involve your child in the preparation of the invitations.

Study item: information needed for party invitations

- Where will the party be held?
- Who is holding the party?
- Is there a special reason for the party?
- Who is being invited?
- What time will the party start and end?
- Is any other information needed?

We all refer to instructions regularly. Let your child see you checking how to put a piece of furniture together, operate a piece of kitchen equipment, and so on. Go through the instructions with her and let her see that you are relying on them. When you play games with her, go through the written rules together first. When she is accustomed to reading and acting upon instructions, see if she can prepare simple written instructions herself. Test her by trying to follow the instructions and discussing how effective they were afterwards.

ENGLISH TESTS FOR SIX- AND SEVEN-YEAR-OLDS

Study item: types of instructions

- Rules of different games.
- Directions showing how to get to different places.
- Instructions as to how to use a telephone.
- Instructions as to how to use a video recorder.
- Suggestions for looking after a pet.
- Steps for locating hidden treasure.

By the time she is seven your child can start keeping simple diaries. This practice will provide valuable experience in working out the most important events in a day. At this stage it will be best to keep the diary going for short periods only, perhaps to mark the highlights of a holiday, or something similar.

You can also encourage your child to read simple poems. Her teacher will be doing this at school, but anything you can do to help at home will be appreciated by the school. Short, simple poems, preferably humorous, are best at this age. Talk about them to your child and see what she thinks of them. Provide her with experiences which involve studying the poems and making decisions about them.

Study item: completing poems

- Choose a word from the group below which will fit into the space:

  Simple Simon met a pieman
  Going to the lake.
  Simple Simon asked the pieman
  "How much is that _____?"

  fake hake cake quake rake

Writing for audiences

As well as expecting your child to be able to write an interesting, creative story, the examiners will also be looking for some sort of evidence that she is beginning to appreciate the scope of language enough to be able to use it sufficiently well to write for different sorts of readers.

As you go through different forms of writing with your child, make sure that she knows the purpose of what she is writing and for whom she is writing it. If you can get her to think on these lines it will become easier for her to adapt her form of writing for its purpose and intention. Ask her to try to assess and analyse different forms of writing in this way.

Study item: writing for audiences

Type of writing	Audience it is meant for	Way it is written
Story (*Cinderella*)	Everyone	In an interesting manner, with fascinating people in it, and a beginning, middle and ending.
Diary	Myself	Short, with only facts and events important to me.
List (*things to buy*)	Mum	Short, single words or groups of words, meant to remind Mum what I want.
Message (*I have gone to my friend's house*)	Parents	A few very brief sentences to provide necessary information.

Grammar and punctuation

Your child's school will be spending a lot of time and trouble in order to bring her up to the appropriate levels of grammar and punctuation. You should need to do relatively little at home. If you can emphasise that sentences begin with capital letters and end with full stops, that should be sufficient. Go through simple sentences in books with your child, pointing out the placement of the capital letters and full stops. Encourage her to make up and write down her own sentences.

Spelling

Your child will be expected by the examiners to be developing as an independent speller at this stage. To reach Level 1 she should be able to spell correctly simple words of one syllable. To be graded Level 2 she ought to be able to go one stage further and spell words with more than one syllable in them. In the spelling test she may be given a story or passage to read and asked to fill in certain spaces with the right words, spelling them correctly.

The best way in which you can supplement the work of the teacher at home is by giving your child certain basic exercises to carry out, to get her used to the sights of words and combinations of letters. With most children, the more practice they get with reading words, the better they become at spelling. Ask her to read the words, say what they mean and copy them down. Any simple words will help your child, but try to give them to her in patterns – short words ending with the same letter, or short words with the same letter in the middle.

Study item: spelling

- words ending in *e*:
  be he me we
- words with *e* in them:
  sea flea real seat eat neat pea tea lean
- words with *ee* in them:
  deep teeth bleed beef seen feed need peel green
- words with *a* in them:
  bat cat fat hat mat pat rat sat

Encourage your child to look for different combinations of words in her reading and to make lists of these words and spell them.

Handwriting

If your child is going to reach Level 3 in English she must be able to use joined handwriting. However, it is essential that you liaise with the school over this. Your child's teacher will have a very careful plan for each of the children in her class, according to their individual needs. She will know just when your child will be ready to be introduced to joined handwriting.

Mention this to the teacher at an open evening at the school and ask if there is anything you can do at home to back up the handwriting activities taking place in the classroom. Do not embark upon any handwriting projects at home without the knowledge and approval of the teacher. To attempt to do so could cause much more harm than good.

ENGLISH TEST – KEY STAGE 1

Your child should read this story herself and answer the questions without help.

Reading comprehension

Read this story and answer the questions about it.

Time: 45 minutes

The Fox Without a Tail

There was once a fox who lost his tail in a trap. This made him very unhappy, because he thought he looked silly.

For a long time the fox did not go home. He spent some time with the badgers but they were too big and slow for him.

ENGLISH TESTS FOR SIX- AND SEVEN-YEAR-OLDS

Then he went to live on the river bank with the water rats, but he did not like the water, so he moved away.

He tried to spend some time outside a town, stealing chickens from coops, but men with guns chased him away.

In the end he went back home to live with the other foxes.

He tried all the time to make all the other foxes lose their tails as well. "If you do that," he said, "you will look much better."

The other foxes just laughed at him. "If you think that," they said, "then why are you so unhappy because you have lost your tail? We like our tails and intend to keep them."

(Aesop)

1 Which animal lost his tail?
   a fox   a dog   a cat   a cow

2 The fox was unhappy because he thought he looked
   sad   thin   silly   angry

3 Why did the fox not like the badgers?
   they were ugly   they were big and slow
   they were old

4 Who did the fox live with on the river bank?
   moles   geese   seagulls   water rats

5 What did the fox dislike about the river bank?
the noise the smell the water the people

6 What did the fox steal from coops?
chickens swans sheep ducks

7 He went back to see
a wizard other foxes a doctor friends

8 He wanted them to
come to a party comfort him cry lose their tails

9 The other foxes
played laughed said nothing ran away

10 Did the other foxes give up their tails?

11 If not, what reason did they give for keeping their tails?

12 Which words in the story begin with the letter *b*?

13 Which words in the story begin with the first letter of the alphabet?

14 Put these words in the order in which they would come in a dictionary.
trap fox lose silly

15 Which word in the story means *sad*?

If the fox without a tail could write, he might have kept the following diary about his movements:

January 1st:	lost tail in trap
January 2nd–January 3rd:	stayed with badgers
January 4th–January 7th:	lived on bank of river
January 8th–January 11th:	lived outside town
January 12th:	returned home

16 On what date did the fox lose his tail?

17 On which dates did he live with the badgers?

18 On which dates did he live on the river bank?

19 What was the last day he lived outside the town?

20 On what date did he return home?

Time: 25 minutes

Living Things

There are different kinds of animals.
There are ways of telling them apart.

Mammals have hair and the young feed on their mother's milk.

Birds have two wings and two feet and feathers, but they do not all fly. Most of them build nests.

Insects have six legs.

Fish have gills to help them breathe in the water and fins which help them to swim.

1 What do mammals have on their
   bodies?
   feathers   spots   hair   lice

2 What do young mammals feed on?
   mother's milk   insects   birds   eggs

3 What is it that not all birds do?
   sing   lay eggs   fly   mate

4 How many legs do insects have?
   eight   four   six   ten

5 What help fish breathe in the water?
   lungs   gills   fins   mouths

6 What help fish to swim?
   gills   fins   arms   legs

7 What covering do birds have on their
   bodies?
   hair   fur   wool   feathers

8 What things do birds have two of?
   heads   wings   eggs   nests

9 What do most birds build?
   houses   barns   boxes   nests

10 How many different kinds of animals
   are described in the piece?
   six   four   eight   three

Spelling and Handwriting

Time: 30 minutes

Write out this piece, putting in the missing words and spelling them correctly. Use your best handwriting. If you can do joined writing, use that.

The Shepherd

A shepherd lost his s_____ and went to l_____ for them. He f_____ them half-way up a h_____. At first they would not c_____ back with him. After a time they s_____ who he was. Then they j_____ up and down happily, because they were g_____ to see him. On the way back they walked s_____. Then they saw their home and s_____ to run quickly.

Writing

Time: 30 minutes

Write a story based on the following event.

You are crossing a field on your way home from school. Suddenly there is a great noise ahead of you. The top of the soil breaks. Slowly, a dinosaur comes out of the earth.

What happens next?

Give your story a title.

Remember that your story should have a *beginning*, a *middle* and an *end*.

Test answers

Reading comprehension
(One mark for each correct answer)

The fox without a tail
1 Fox
2 Silly
3 They were big and slow.
4 Water rats
5 Water
6 Chickens
7 Other foxes
8 Lose their tails
9 Laughed
10 No
11 They liked their tails.
12 Because, badgers, big, but, back, better (in any order)
13 are, a, all, as, away, at (in any order)
14 Fox, lose, silly, trap (in this order)
15 Unhappy
16 January 1st
17 January 2nd and 3rd
18 January 4th, 5th, 6th, 7th
19 January 11th
20 January 12th
  (Total: 20)

Living things
1 Hair
2 Mother's milk
3 Fly
4 Six
5 Gills
6 Fins
7 Feathers

8 Wings and feet

9 Nests

10 Four
(Total: 10)

Spelling (One mark for each correct answer)

1 Sheep

2 Look

3 Found

4 Hill

5 Come

6 Saw

7 Jumped

8 Glad

9 Slowly

10 Started
(Total: 10)

Handwriting

This must be subjective. If you wish to try to assess this remember that to achieve Level 3 and above the handwriting should be joined, legible and attractive. A suggested marking scheme out of 10 is:

not joined, letters different sizes, generally untidy	4
not joined, letters the same, sizes, generally tidy	5
joined, letters different sizes, generally tidy	7
joined, letters same sizes, generally tidy	8
joined, tidy, attractive to look at	9
faultless!	10

Story writing

Again, this must be subjective. A suggested marking scheme out of 20 is:

	Mark range
An attempt to write something connected to the theme set, with a title which is not too irrelevant, sketchy grasp of characterisation and a not very interesting attempt at a flowing story, with poor use of full stops and capital letters.	0–5
Basic simple story line with title which bears some connection to contents, not too well constructed but with a definite beginning and ending, with some attempt to construct sentences with full stops and capital letters.	5–10
Interesting story, not too well organised but leading to a definite climax, with characters who can be told apart, with an appropriate title, written in cohesive sentences with generally suitable use of capital letters and full stops.	10–15
Interesting and imaginative story with arresting start, relevant title, well-defined characters and a pronounced beginning, middle and end, written in sentences with appropriate use of full stops, capital letters and grammar.	15–20

Gradings

Give one mark for each correct answer in the reading and spelling tests, and give an appropriate score from the grading columns for handwriting and story writing.

ENGLISH TESTS FOR SIX- AND SEVEN-YEAR-OLDS

Ratings for reading comprehension

Marks	Level	Rating
22–30	3	above average
12–22	2	average
0–12	1	below average

Ratings for spelling

Marks	Level	Rating
7–10	3	above average
3–7	2	average
0–3	1	below average

Ratings for handwriting

Marks	Level	Rating
7–10	3	above average
3–7	2	average
0–3	1	below average

Ratings for story writing

Marks	Level	Rating
15–20	3	above average
8–14	2	average
0–7	1	below average

Overall English ratings

Marks	Level	Rating
51–70	3	above average
26–50	2	average
0–25	1	below average

Parents talking

     ❝ One drawback to working with your child at home is that he soon begins to realise that you don't have all the answers all the time. Frankly, I think I'm beginning to be a bit of a disappointment to him. ❞

     ❝ On the whole I enjoy working at home with my children, but after a particularly bad evening I start to wonder whether there might be less exacting ways of our being miserable together. ❞

Useful books at Key Stage 1

Parents

Handwriting – the way to teach it, Rosemary Sassoon, Leopard Learning.

Help your child with reading and writing, Lesley Clark, Positive Parenting series, Headway, Hodder and Stoughton.

Inspirations for English, Helen Hadley, Scholastic.

Children

Assessment Papers English 7–8 years, J. M. Bond, Nelson.

Back to Basics English Books 1 and 2, Sheila Lane and Marion Kemp, Letts.

Writing for a Purpose, Jane Whitwell and Norma Gaunt, Scholastic.

Collins Primary Dictionary, Collins.

CHAPTER FOUR

Mathematics tests for six- and seven-year-olds

Doing sums

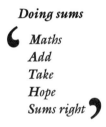

> *Maths*
> *Add*
> *Take*
> *Hope*
> *Sums right*

Billy, aged seven

At the age of seven your child will take two mathematics test papers. The first one will be to see if he has reached the basic Level 1. The results of the second test paper will determine whether he has reached the average Level 2, or the above average Level 3. A child of outstanding ability will be given an extra paper to see if he can reach the standard normally attained by eleven-year-olds – Level 4.

These papers will cover a number of branches of mathematics. There will be an emphasis on *number*, the basic use of figures and how to recognise and use them, especially with the four rules. This is the name given to addition, subtraction, multiplication and division. About 70 per cent of the test questions for seven-year-olds will be concerned with number.

Your child will also be expected to be developing an understanding of *shape, space and measures*. Basically he will be expected to have some knowledge of patterns and shapes and how to measure them.

Your child should be able to use his knowledge of mathematics and apply it to everyday problems and situations. He may also be asked to demonstrate that he can recognise and use simple charts and graphs.

Using and applying mathematics

As your child learns more about mathematics he will be expected to show that he appreciates that there is a reason for acquiring such knowledge and skills. Emphasis should be placed on counting and using the four rules in practical situations.

What the examiners will be looking for

The questions will be designed to see whether your child can use the four rules in practical situations, perform basic calculations with numbers, sort objects into groups, check answers to sums, and recognise and measure different shapes.

To be graded at Level 1, a child should be able to discuss what he is doing, draw pictures to show what he has accomplished and be able to recognise simple patterns and relationships.

A child attaining the average grading of Level 2 will be expected to select the appropriate sort of mathematics needed to solve an everyday problem. He should also be able to use simple diagrams and symbols. If he is asked, 'What would happen if . . .' in a mathematical context at a basic level, he should know what to do next.

An above average child reaching Level 3 should be capable of trying different approaches to problems and overcoming difficulties which might arise. He should be able to organise his work and explain what he is doing.

Studying the use and application of mathematics at home

You will not have to do much at home in order to get your child used to handling mathematics. It is, however, important to be consistent. Give your child regular practice for about 30 minutes once a week over a period of a year with the activities described in this section. Start at the beginning of Year 2, in September, and by the time your child takes the tests towards the end of that school year he should have had enough useful experience to acquit himself well in the tests.

At this formative stage you can give your child a great deal of assistance if you play games with him which involve recognising and using figures and counting numbers. These activities could include playing such games as 'Ludo' and 'Snakes and Ladders', in which the child has to throw a dice and then count along the board. Help him with the counting at first and then, as he grows more confident, allow him to do his own counting, intervening only when he makes a mistake. If this happens, get him to check his counting. If the game involves adding up scores, include your child in this as well.

Remember that you are preparing your child for written tests, so take every opportunity to encourage him to write down the results of his mathematical thinking.

One of the most practical ways of experiencing mathematics is by using money. Any experience with coins will serve to reinforce your child's understanding that mathematics can be used for practical purposes. Give your child plenty of small change and give him various problems to solve, asking him to write down the answers.

Study item: making up

- Use real coins for making up numbers, i.e. how many different ways can 10p be made up?
  (Answer: 5p + 5p, 1p + 9p, etc.)
- As your child's knowledge of figures grows, ask him to make up increasingly large sums – 50p, 60p, and so on.

- From this it will be possible to go on to other practical aspects of mathematics – adding and subtracting coins, giving change, etc.

You can also show your child how to compare weights and distances, introducing him to the terms *heavier than, lighter than,* and *shorter than, longer than.* Remember to get him accustomed to writing answers down.

Study item: comparisons of weight

- Make a collection of small objects of different weights – bars of chocolate, small jars, etc. Give two different objects to your child at a time and ask him to judge which is the heavier, and to write down his findings.
- Let him see you check the results by weighing the items on scales, to accustom him to the idea that weight may be ascertained. Later, let him use the scales himself as he becomes more proficient.
- As he gains in confidence give your child three different objects and ask him to compare weights, using the terms *lighter than* and *heavier than.* For example, 'This box is heavier than that jar, but it is lighter than this parcel.'

Study item: comparisons of length

- Collect small objects of different lengths. Put them in pairs and ask your child to estimate which is the longest and write down what he thinks.
- Help him check the lengths. First use non-standard measures, like finger-tips, forearms, etc.
- When you child has gained enough experience, check the estimates with standard measures – rulers, tape-measures, etc.

Any practical help which you can give your child with time will pay dividends when it comes to taking the tests.

MATHEMATICS TESTS FOR SIX- AND SEVEN-YEAR-OLDS

Study item: time

- Start estimating and comparing time – 'that song lasted longer than this one.' 'It took me longer to walk round the garden than it did to climb the stairs.'
- Take part in activities which involve using the words quick and slow.
- Learn how to tell the time, first the hours only, and then minutes.
- Start to estimate the length of time something will take, and then check it by timing it with a watch.
- Solve problems involving the passage of time – 'If a job takes 30 minutes and ends at 5 o'clock, at what time will it have started?'

Number

Most of the test papers at this level will be concerned with aspects of number, so it is important that your child can recognise numerals up to 100, and can add, subtract, multiply and divide.

What the examiners will be looking for

If a child is to be assessed as being at Level 1, the below average score for this age, he should be capable of reading and recognising numbers up to ten and of counting, adding and subtracting them in simple problems.

An average child, at Level 2, should be able to group objects in sets, add and subtract mentally and understand place values – units, tens and hundreds – up to 100. He should know the difference between odd and even numbers. He should be able to work confidently when adding and subtracting up to 100. He should also be able to recognise halves and quarters of numbers and objects.

An above average child, able to reach Level 3, should be capable of recognising numbers up to 1000. He should also be able to add and subtract mentally with numbers up to 20. He should be able to use the 2×, 5× and 10× tables in solving multiplication and division problems. He should be able to add and subtract two-digit numbers, and use a calculator to check answers. He should be beginning to use decimals.

Studying number at home

Give your child as much practice as possible in writing down and recognising numbers. Start with 1 to 10 and then proceed in easy stages up to 100. If your child can familiarise himself with these numbers then he is well on the way to doing well in the Key Stage 1 tests. If he seems particularly adept at this, go on until he can recognise numbers up to 1000, but do not rush it.

When you are sure that your child is familiar with the shape of all the numbers from one to 100, ascertain that he can put each number in its correct place. Write the numbers down in order and leave some gaps. Make sure that your child can fill in the right numbers. Number patterns, as these are known, often come up in the test papers.

Study item: number patterns

- Fill in these gaps:
  26 27 __ 29 30 __ 32 __
- Do at least one set of number patterns every week, increasing the numbers until they become familiar to your child and he can fill one in without difficulty.

Your child's teacher will be concentrating on basic addition and subtraction and making sure that he knows his 2×, 5× and 10× tables, and probably the 3× and 4× as well. You can do some sums and tables of this nature at home, but at this stage it will be of more use if you help your child understand place value.

This is the value of each digit in a number. At Key Stage 1, children should be able to recognise tens and units up to 100.

MATHEMATICS TESTS FOR SIX- AND SEVEN-YEAR-OLDS

Study item: tens and units

•	18		26		34		61	
	Tens	Units	Tens	Units	Tens	Units	Tens	Units
	1	8	2	6	3	4	6	1

Study item: place value

- Underline the tens in each of the numbers below:
  56   24   32   45   18
- Underline the units in each of the numbers below:
  32   57   12   16   86

If your child enjoys this work and does well at it, give him the chance to recognise hundreds, tens and units in the same way.

You should also introduce your child to the use of a calculator, making sure that he can turn it on and off and generally handle it.

Shape, space and measures

Your child will be expected to take an interest in shape and movement and be able to carry out simple measuring techniques.

What the examiners will be looking for

At the very basic Level 1 standard, the examiners will be looking for signs that a child can carry out elementary measuring, can recognise the difference between flat two-dimensional shapes and three-dimensional shapes, and can use everyday language to explain the position and shapes of objects.

The average child at Level 2 should be able to recognise and describe sides and corners, distinguish between straight and turning movements, understand that an angle is a measurement of a turn and be able to recognise a right angle in a turn. He should be able to carry out simple measurements.

At Level 3, the above average child will be expected in addition to describe and classify 2D and 3D shapes, understand symmetry and be able to measure length, capacity, mass and time.

Studying shape, space and measures at home

In order to help your child do well in this section of the mathematics tests you should help him to concentrate on different shapes and ways of moving.

The best way to start is by encouraging your child to make his own patterns, so that he can appreciate what one is. Ask him to use building blocks and make patterns by colour – red-blue-red-blue, etc. These patterns can get more involved and intricate in time. Ask him to look for examples of patterns around him, in such objects as tiles, carpets, wallpaper, and so on. Make collections of patterns in nature, including those on leaves and flowers.

Study item: movement

- Use a piece of cardboard as a race track and make up a game with a toy motor car, moving it in different directions.
- If you do not move the car in the right direction as soon as it is called out, you will lose a point.
- How many other games involving movement can you think of?

Show him the difference between three-dimensional and two-dimensional shapes and encourage him to handle 3D building blocks and other similar objects. Count and record the number of sides the different objects have. Copy these shapes and make others out of modelling clay. Collect examples of 2D shapes and group them under headings – straight, curved, pointed, etc.

Study item: 2D and 3D shapes

- Examine boxes and cut the sides from them. Stick the sides on to a piece of cardboard. How many sides does each box have?
- Does each 3D shape have the same number of sides?

Ask your child to work out why man-made objects are the shape they are. Why are mugs made in a particular way? Why do teapots have spouts?

Study item: shapes

- Make a study of animal camouflage. Look at pictures of different animals in their habitats.
- Why do some animals have skins of a particular colour or pattern? Give examples of this.
- What other practical uses are there for shapes and patterns?

Explain the difference between odd and even numbers and ask your child to write down examples of both. Play games like dominoes and noughts and crosses, which involve both shapes and movement.

Study item: odd and even numbers

- Construct the shapes of even numbers, using matchsticks or building blocks.
- Construct the shapes of odd numbers, using matchsticks or building blocks.

Begin to experiment with capacity and volume. Estimate and then check how many cups of water it will take to fill a jug. How many dried peas will it take to fill a small jar?

Study item: capacity and volume

- Conduct a study to see if containers which look the same size hold the same amounts of liquid.
- Present your answers in pictorial shape.

Encourage your child to look for signs near the house and to copy them down. What is the purpose of each sign? What shape is it? Start learning the names of such basic shapes as square, circle, triangle and rectangle. Collect examples of each and label them.

Study item: shapes

- Make patterns involving all the 2D shapes you have learnt about – squares, circles, etc.
- Make patterns involving different 3D shapes – tins, boxes, building blocks, etc.

HELP YOUR CHILD WITH THE NATIONAL CURRICULUM TESTS

MATHEMATICS TEST – KEY STAGE 1

Number

Time: 40 minutes

1 6
  3+
	2 4
	  2+
		3 5
		  4+
			4 7
			  1+
				5 2
				  6+

6 8
  5
  3+
	7 5
	  3
	  4+
		8 7
		  2
		  6+
			9 6
			  4
			  2+
				10 3
				  5
				  6+

11 8
  2–
	12 10
	  4–
		13 9
		  3–
			14 4
			  2–
				15 7
				  4–

16 11
  5–
	17 12
	  4–
		18 13
		  3–
			19 14
			  6–
				20 15
				  9–

In the numbers below, which figures are tens?

21 21 22 34 23 46 24 52 25 76
26 111 27 456 28 754 29 194 30 567

In the numbers below, which figures are units?

31 41 32 43 33 25 34 14 35 67
36 234 37 101 38 984 39 385 40 267

41 What is half of 44?
42 What is half of 26?
43 What is half of 12?
44 What is a quarter of 4?
45 What is a quarter of 12?
46 What is a quarter of 8?
47 Which of the numbers below are even numbers?

4   7   10   15   16   20

48 Which of the numbers below are odd numbers?

1   2   4   7   9   10

49 Finish off this number pattern:

123   456   ___

50 12 × 5 =

Using and applying mathematics

Time: 10 minutes

1 If school starts at 9.00 a.m., what time would you have to get there to be five minutes early?

2 If you have 50p and buy two toys, each costing 20p, how much change will you have?

Shape, space and measures

Time: 30 minutes

How many sides does each of these figures have?

1   **2**

3 Put a cross where each angle is on this figure.

4 Complete this drawing so that you have a figure which is symmetrical.

5 Measure your handspan and say how wide it is.

6 Write down the names of any three objects which are square in shape.

7 Measure each of these lines. How long are they?

    (a) ——————————————

    (b) ——————

    (c) ——————————————————

8 Write down half of the length of each of the three lines in question 7.

Test answers

Number

1 9	**2** 6	**3** 9	**4** 8	**5** 8	**6** 16	**7** 12	**8** 15	**9** 12
10 14	**11** 6	**12** 6	**13** 6	**14** 2	**15** 3	**16** 6	**17** 8	
18 10	**19** 8	**20** 6	**21** 2	**22** 3	**23** 4	**24** 5	**25** 7	
26 1	**27** 5	**28** 5	**29** 9	**30** 6	**31** 1	**32** 3	**33** 5	
34 4	**35** 7	**36** 4	**37** 1	**38** 4	**39** 5	**40** 7	**41** 22	
42 13	**43** 6	**44** 1	**45** 3	**46** 2	**47** 4, 10, 16, 20			
48 1, 7, 9	**49** 789		**50** 60					

(Total: 50)

Using and applying mathematics

1 8.55 (or 5 minutes to 9)
2 10p
(Total: 2)

Shape, space and measures

1 4
2 3
3 One cross on each join.
4

5 Check child's handspan.
6 Give one mark for any three sensible answers.
7 (*a*) 4 cm, (*b*) 2 cm, (*c*) 5 cm
8 (*a*) 2 cm, (*b*) 1 cm, (*c*) 2.5 cm.
(Total: 8)

Gradings

Give one mark for each correct answer.

Number

Marks	Level	Rating
35–50	3	above average
20–35	2	average
0–20	1	below average

Shape, space and measures

Marks	Level	Rating
5–8	3	above average
3–5	2	average
0–2	1	below average

Overall mathematics gradings

Marks	Level	Rating
40–60	3	above average
23–40	2	average
0–22	1	below average

Parents talking

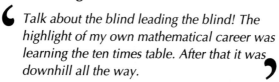

Talk about the blind leading the blind! The highlight of my own mathematical career was learning the ten times table. After that it was downhill all the way.

I really admire teachers these days. At least they taught my son to read. I can't even teach him to think.

Useful books at Key Stage 1

Parents

Help your child with maths, Sue Atkinson, Positive Parenting series, Headway, Hodder and Stoughton.
Back to basics – Core Subjects, Graeme Kent, Pearson.
Inspirations for Maths, Beryl Webber and Jean Haigh, Scholastic.

Children

Numbers to 20, Rose Griffiths, Essential for Maths series, Scholastic.
Maths Games, Lynne Burgess, Scholastic

CHAPTER FIVE

English tests for ten- and eleven-year-olds

My favourite words

❛ *astronomy trilling extravagance tulip landscape masterpiece fishing determine consequence karate* ❜

Chris, aged ten

When your child reaches the age of eleven she will be tested in these aspects of English:

- Reading
- Writing (including Handwriting and Spelling).

Your child will be assessed and marked in each of these sub-sections before she is given an overall English grade.

READING

The reading tests are designed to see how well your child can read, understand and respond to different forms of writing – stories, articles, poems and factual information.

In the test your child will be given a booklet containing a

number of examples of varying types of writing. These may include a story, a poem and several factual accounts or articles. Your child will be given 15 minutes to read through the booklet. She will then be asked to answer certain questions about its various contents. These questions are provided in a separate booklet which she will be asked to fill in. She will be allowed 45 minutes for this.

The teacher will read aloud the first questions, which are examples, and your child and the others in the class will work through the answers between them, to make sure that they understand what they have to do. Then each child will be told to carry on working through the answer booklet on her own.

The story

The story will be by a well-known writer of children's fiction and will be both interesting and well written.

What the examiners will be looking for

The questions on the story will be divided into four main sections, each devised to test your child's ability to understand and assess:

1 questions about the characters
2 questions about the story
3 questions about the way in which the story is written
4 questions about the reader's opinion of the story.

The average child will receive a grading at Level 4 and will be expected to show reasonable reading ability and be able to answer most of the factual questions about the story, but may not be as sensitive in assessing character development or be so skilled in articulating her opinion of aspects of the story.

A child almost approaching this level will be regarded as slightly below average and will be rated at Level 3. The standards expected at Level 3 have been dealt with in Chapter 3.

A child obtaining the above average grading of Level 5 should display good reading skills and be able to assess both the quality of a story and the main intentions of the writer.

The standards expected at Level 6 will be found in Chapter 8.

Studying the story test at home

Encourage your child to continue reading as many different kinds of story books as possible. If at this stage you can encourage her to share her thoughts and opinions of the book she reads, you will be helping her greatly and preparing her for the tests she will be taking. Ask her questions about what she has read in order to make sure that she understands the stories. In this year's tests the examiners are keen to analyse the children's personal responses to the stories provided, so it will benefit her enormously if your child gets into the habit of assessing what she has read.

Characters

It is important at this stage that she takes an interest in the characters in the story – who they are, what they do and how they relate to one another. If she can learn to assess and describe characters, and say what they *are*, it will help her reach Level 4 standard. If she can go a little farther and *relate* characters to one another, and give reasons for their actions, this will put your child in the above average class and give her a chance of reaching Level 5 or Level 6. In order to do this, and to familiarise your child with the requisite skills, there are a few simple exercises with which you can assist her at home.

Assessing characters in stories

In order to make such assessments second nature it will help if she is asked to compile her own character sheets about the people or creatures in the stories she reads. After your child has finished reading a book ask her, as a matter of course, to provide five adjectives which will describe each of the main protagonists in the story.

Study item: character assessment test (1)

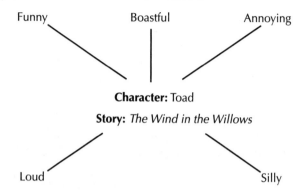

Study item: character assessment test (2)

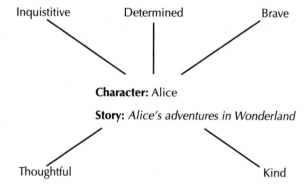

The questions

Your child will be asked a number of straightforward questions about the events in the story she is given to read for the test. Impress upon her the necessity to read the questions carefully, so that she will know what is expected of her.

ENGLISH TESTS FOR TEN- AND ELEVEN-YEAR-OLDS

This should be an easy section of the test paper for most children, so it is important that the maximum amount of marks be obtained from it. The format for the questions will usually be that of the *multiple choice* variety. In other words, after the question has been asked four possible answers will be given. Your child will be asked to draw a ring round the answer which she thinks is correct.

You can best help here by giving your child tests of this sort on what she has just read. Prepare about ten questions for each story, and give four possible answers for each question. In order to make your child think things through, make sure that there is a touch of logic to each possible answer. Do not make any of the answers wildly improbable, or your child will find the exercise too easy.

Study item: test on Cinderella

- Where did Cinderella want to go?
  to a party   to a ball   to a show   to a disco
- Who would not let Cinderella leave home?
  her sisters   her brother   her father   her friends

Ways in which the story is written

Your child will be asked some questions about the ways in which the story in the test has been written. These questions will focus on the use of language in the story and upon the meanings of some of the phrases used by the writer to make an effect.

Your child's teacher should be spending a lot of time on this part of the test, so you will not need to do a great deal at home. A form of language often found in this test is the use of the *simile*. A simile is an imaginative comparison involving the use of the word *as* or *like*, for example, *the tablecloth was as white as snow*, or *the cat stretched like a piece of elastic being pulled slowly*.

Encourage your child to look for similes in her own reading and to try to make up her own examples. This will familiarise her with the process and help her to understand the meanings of the similes she might be asked to explain in the test.

Study item: complete these similes

The dog pounced like _____.

The girl yawned like _____.

The frog jumped like _____.

The sea was as blue as _____.

The giant was as big as _____.

The plain was as empty as _____.

The pain was as sharp as _____.

Opinions on the story

Those children who are prepared to work hard and accept help from their parents and teachers ought to be able to proceed through the sections on the characters and the story in the English test without too much difficulty. The more complex part will be completing the section asking for opinions on the story.

At this age many children lack confidence in their own ability, and when asked to depart from strictly factual answers they tend to give a perfunctory response. This is a pity, because a few extra marks obtained in this section of the paper may make the difference between an average Level 4 rating and a superior grading at Level 5 or Level 6.

As always, the child who reads most at home for her own enjoyment will have the best chance of working through this part of the paper with confidence and enjoyment.

Continue to urge your child to read as many stories as she can. Talk to her about them and pay particular attention to the following aspects of the stories, as these tend to be the areas dealt with most prominently in the test.

- Opinion of the story.
- Title of the story.
- Identification with the story.

Opinion of the story

In some form or other your child will almost certainly be asked if she likes the story or not. More importantly, she will be asked *why* she liked or disliked it. Answers to the second part of the nature of 'It was good' or 'It was scary' would not receive high marks for perceptive analysis, even at this young age.

When you discuss the book she has read, encourage your child to give her instinctive opinion as to whether she liked it or not, and then, over a period of time, encourage her to give the reasons for her opinion under a certain number of headings. If you do this with all the books she reads in the run-up to the test it should become second nature to her to analyse stories in this way, and so give a reasoned answer to the question in the test paper.

Give your child practice in saying what she thinks of the books she reads under the headings of *story, characters, writing, setting, subject* and *ending*. If she wishes to discuss other aspects of the book as well this should be encouraged, once the basic assessments have been made, although it must be remembered that in this section of the paper there will only be room for short answers, perhaps between twenty and thirty words in some cases.

Study item: what I think of the book
Title of book _____

The story	The characters	The writing
exciting interesting believable funny, etc	well drawn recognisable good company, etc	lively understandable, etc

Why I liked or disliked the book

The setting	The subject	The ending
fascinating dramatic recognisable unusual, etc	well known different, etc	satisfying enjoyable, etc

Title of the story

Help your child to think about the titles of the stories she reads, as she may well be asked to consider this aspect in the test paper. She may be asked whether or not she considers the title a suitable one, or to suggest another appropriate title for the story.

Emphasise that a title has a number of functions. It should be interesting or dramatic, it should deal with an important aspect of the story, and preferably it should be short.

When you are discussing the story your child has read ask her if she can think of another title for it. Make a short-list of titles and decide between you which is the most appropriate.

Study item: alternative titles

Title:	*Little Red Riding Hood*
Alternative titles:	*The Big Bad Wolf*
	Death of a Grandmother
	A Strange Visit
	Who's in that Bed?

Identification with the story

At this stage of the test your child may well be asked to show her knowledge and appreciation of the story by saying what she might have done in the same circumstances.

Study item: *Robinson Crusoe*

- How well would you do on your own on an island?
- What would you do to try to keep alive?

When you talk to your child about the book she has read put her in the position of the hero or heroine and ask her how she would cope if faced with the same difficulties, until you get her accustomed to identifying with the problems posed in the books she reads.

The articles

The questions about the articles will be factual ones about the contents of the pieces. Sometimes your child will be asked to quote the actual words from the articles which provide the answers to the question. If there are two articles about the same subject, she may be asked questions about similarities or differences between the descriptions.

What the examiners will be looking for

A child who can answer factual questions on the contents of the articles or reports and can go on to draw conclusions from these facts and display knowledge of how to obtain further information will be regarded as above average and rated at Level 6. A child approaching this standard will be considered to be at Level 5.

To reach Level 4, the average standard, a child should be able to answer most of the factual questions and be able to work out some of the conclusions to be drawn from these answers. To reach Level 3 a child will show that she is close to this standard.

Studying the non-fiction writing test at home

The object of this section of the test paper is to see how well children can respond to factual or non-chronological writing. The essence of this sort of writing is that it has to put over information in as short and succinct a form as possible. Children reading it must learn to extract the salient points from the material and show that they understand it.

The best way to help your child to do this at home is by showing her plenty of examples of different kinds of non-chronological writing – labels, announcements, instructions, recipes, rules, advertisements, directions, etc. Ask her to read these different forms and to say, in as few words as possible, what each one is about and what information it is intended to convey.

As a rule in the tests the children will be asked to answer two forms of questions. One of these types will require them to use their own words in order to provide the answer. The second type of question will ask them to quote the actual words in the passage which will provide the answer.

Study item: instructions

To start the lawnmower, pull the starter cord. Do not tilt the lawnmower at this stage. Do not put your hands near the rotating parts. Hold the steering bar firmly.

Questions

1 How do you start the lawnmower?
2 Write down the sentence which tells you what not to do with the lawnmower at this stage.
3 What does the word *rotating* mean?

When you question your child about the factual material she is reading, give her both kinds of questions – those which require a general understanding of the material and those which ask for a specific phrase or sentence from the material.

In this section of the paper your child may also be asked to demonstrate that she knows how to seek out information by going to the right sources. Make sure that she knows which sorts of books to go to for specific information. Give her books of this sort as well as simple but specific research tasks such as finding an address, etc. Make sure that she knows how to use chapter headings and indexes.

Study item: information books

directories	dictionaries	atlases
recipes	instructions	timetables
encyclopaedias	guide books	programmes
manuals		

The poem

The questions about the poem will be intended to test your child's knowledge of its content and meaning.

What the examiners will be looking for

At Level 4, the average child will show by her answers that she understands the meaning of the poem, and is able to draw her own conclusions, based on this understanding.

To be rated at Level 5, the above average grading, a child will have to show that she can answer questions about the content of the poem, make deductions from information provided in the poem, and demonstrate an understanding of the meaning of the language used.

Children still graded at Levels 1 or 2 will be individually assessed by the teacher before receiving their ratings.

Studying the poetry test at home

Encourage your child to read plenty of poems, those you and she both like and a selection from the reading list provided at the end of this chapter. By questioning, make sure that she understands what the poems are about. In the test the opening questions will be multiple choice questions about the contents of the poem, so see that your child has had a number of opportunities of choosing between possible answers before she takes the test.

Study item: *Peter, Peter, Pumpkin Eater*

Peter, Peter, pumpkin eater,
Had a wife and couldn't keep her.
He put her in a pumpkin shell,
And there he kept her very well.

- What did Peter have?
  a dog   a house   a friend   a wife
- Where did Peter keep his wife?
  in a palace in a tree   in a pumpkin shell   in a boat

There will also probably be questions to see if your child can deduce facts from the evidence provided in the poem, so ask your child if she can guess the answers to such questions as where the action occurs, what time of year it is, what the weather is like, and so on.

Study item: *There's Snow on the Fields*

There's snow on the fields,
And cold in the cottage,
While I sit in the chimney nook
Supping hot pottage.

- What time of year do you think it is?

The examiners will be hoping that at least some of the children taking the test will display an appreciation and understanding of poetic phrases used in the test piece. The more poetry your child reads the more affinity she is likely to show for the way in which it is written, so when you discuss the poems she has read, ask her to give her own opinions of what certain lines or parts of lines mean.

Study item: *It's Winter*

The leaves said, 'It's winter;
Weary are we.'
So they all lay down and slept
Under the tree.

- What did the leaves really do when the poet said that they lay down and slept under the tree?

WRITING

The writing section of the test will consist of three separate parts:

1 Story writing
2 Spelling
3 Handwriting.

Story writing

The story-writing section of the test will be divided into two parts – *narrative* and *non-narrative*.

Narrative writing

The narrative test will consist of your child being asked to write an imaginative story. To this end she will be provided with a choice of subjects. For each story she will be given a short *starting point*. Usually this will comprise a few words intended to get your child thinking about what she should do. For example

Title: *The Runaway Pet*
Many of us have pets. They can be quite common or rather unusual. Usually they stay with us happily. Write a story about a pet which runs away and has to be looked for.

In addition to the title and a few opening suggestions, the test paper will also contain an outline upon which your child can write a few brief notes in order to plan her short story. These notes will contain spaces for her to jot down the *title* of the story, *where* it takes place, *who* is in the story, and how it *begins*, *develops* and *ends*.

Your child will be allocated 15 minutes to plan her story and jot down these notes to help her. Then 45 minutes will be allowed for the actual writing of the story.

What the examiners will be looking for

At Level 4 the children taking the test should be providing evidence that they are capable of writing an interesting, well-paced story with a recognisable beginning, middle and end. The story should make sense, with recognisable characters who relate to one another. Direct or reported speech should be used to distinguish between the characters. Sentences should be properly structured and there should be signs that the children can make some use of paragraphs.

For the above average grading of Level 5 a child should be able to use grammatical sentences and paragraphs to show believable characters engaged in interesting activities. Dialogue should be used between speech marks.

Children who cannot produce narrative writing of this standard will receive one of the below average scores, depending upon the quality of the work. At the lowest grade, Level 1, a child will only be capable of producing a few words, not always even related to the subject matter. For children considered to be at Levels 1 or 2, and who are obviously finding great difficulty with the test, the teacher will probably give extra assessment on a one-to-one basis in order to grade them accurately.

Studying the narrative writing test at home

You can, of course, use the books your child is reading as examples of what her own writing should aspire to. In particular, study those aspects of the stories which are outlined in the notes provided in the test papers – *title, setting, characters,* and *beginning, development* and *ending.*

Encourage your child to write her own stories, perhaps based on the book she has been reading. Go through them with her afterwards and discuss together how she has treated the main points of the story.

Study item: story checklist

Title: Is the title short and interesting and does it refer to an important aspect of the story?

Characters: Is there a leading character who is the hero or heroine of the story, and does this character come into conflict with another character or some aspect of nature – a storm, getting lost, etc?

Beginning: Does the story begin in an interesting way and take us straight in to the action of the story?

Development: Does the story lead into a number of steps or action points which develop the story and tell us something about the characters?

Ending: Does the story end on a high-point in a manner which satisfies the reader?

There is one extra ingredient of a narrative story of which the examiner will be hoping to catch a glimpse if he is to grade your child at Level 6 or above. This is a *theme*. A theme is the basic idea behind the story, the power which gives a story its thrust. The theme of *Othello* is jealousy, for example.

Of course, no one is going to expect an eleven-year-old child to be thinking this thoroughly about her creative writing, but you could help add an extra dimension to her narrative if, after discussing the other aspects of the story, you could ask her to tell you what the story was about. 'Your story is about some children getting together to help a lost dog, so you are really writing about *consideration* or *kindness.*'

If your child seems to understand this approach, encourage her towards the end of the story to mention the theme to show that she knows what she is doing in her writing activities.

Your child will also be expected to display certain basic technical knowledge of the writing process. Her teacher will be working very hard on this at school, but when you are reading her efforts at home, make sure that she is enhancing them by using sentences and paragraphs.

Study item: sentences and paragraphs

- A sentence begins with a capital letter, ends with a full stop and contains a verb.
- A paragraph contains more than one sentence. It is used whenever a fresh thought or incident is introduced into a story. The first word of a paragraph is set in a few places from the side of the page.

Give your child as much practice as possible in writing direct speech, using speech marks or inverted commas to enclose any dialogue. One way of improving this area of her work is for you to give her examples of indirect speech and ask her to turn it into direct speech.

Study item: direct and indirect speech

- *Indirect speech:*   He said he would come.
- *Direct speech:*   He said, 'I shall come.'
- *Indirect speech:*   She asked where the flowers were.
- *Direct speech:*   'Where are the flowers?' she asked.

Non-narrative writing

In addition to writing a story your child will also be asked to write something factual. This might be a letter or a report of some kind.

Again, she will be given help with the planning of the writing. This will consist of printed details of what is required, which will also be read out by the teacher. The details will supply the information upon which the letter or report is to be based.

Study item: ideas for non-narrative writing
Sports Day

- A new teacher has arrived at your school and has organised some strange events for Sports Day. Here are some of the new events – there were also others!
  - The digging down to Australia race.
  - Throwing the sausage.
- Write a letter to your Headteacher saying what you thought of the new events, and making suggestions for other events, describing suitable prizes.

There will be a blank piece of paper in the answer book for your child to make notes before writing the letter or making a report. There will also be more detailed suggestions, if your child wishes to use them to help her plan the letter, including a reminder to include the name of the school and the date of the Sports Day, and such ideas as those shown below.

Study item: notes

- Describe the unusual events in detail.
- What happened in these events?

- How did you feel about them?
- How could they be improved?
- What do you feel about Sports Day in general?

What the examiners will be looking for

To attain a Level 4 grading a child should be able to cover the main issues of the piece of writing asked for, begin it in an interesting way and round it off satisfactorily.

With the above average child at Level 5, the examiners will expect detailed, fluent and confident writing which will hold the interest of the reader. There must be definite signs that the child understands what is expected of her and knows what she is trying to put over to the reader. The issues mentioned in the briefing notes will be covered and the construction will be organised and progressive, with the correct use of paragraphs. The final paragraph should summarise and emphasise the main thrust of the piece of writing.

Studying the non-narrative writing test at home

Continue to show your child examples of non-chronological writing – reports, articles, letters, etc – and stress the importance of putting as much information as possible into a confined space.

A good way of getting her into the habit of including only essential facts is by asking her to make lists of the most important items to be included in various reports.

Study item: essential items for inclusion in requirements list for day's walking

- destination
- route
- time of departure
- clothing and footwear required
- food needed
- time of return.

Spelling

The spelling test will consist of another story, with gaps where words have been left out. The context of the piece will make it fairly obvious which words have been omitted. Your child will be asked to fill in the gaps with the correct words, spelling them correctly. This test should take about ten minutes.

Study item spelling test: *Snow White*

Once there was a beautiful young _____ called Snow White. She was the daughter of a king, so she was also a _____. Snow White's mother died and her father married again, so his new wife became the _____ of the country. Snow White became very unhappy and decided to run away from _____.

What the examiners will be looking for

The marking of spelling is an objective affair. One mark will be given for each word spelt correctly. The words will grow progressively more difficult. Children spelling some or all of the first 15 words will be graded at Levels 1 or 2, depending upon the number of correct answers. Children answering the first 15 words correctly and some or all of the next 20 words will be graded between Levels 3 and 6, depending upon the number of correct spellings.

Studying the spelling test at home

The more your child reads the better her grasp of spelling should become. If her teacher sends spelling lists home, help your child to learn the words on the lists. The best way of learning to spell a word is for the child to write it down correctly and then follow this sequence of events.

Study item: learning to spell

- **Saying:**   Look at the word and say it aloud a number of times.

- **Looking:** Look at the word and break it down into syllables, repeating each syllable aloud. Look away and try to spell the word.
- **Recalling:** Look at the word again. Shut your eyes and spell it. If unsuccessful, go through the first three stages again.
- **Writing:** Write down the word from memory. If unsuccessful, go through the first four stages again.
- **Mastering:** Write down the word from memory. If unsuccessful, go through the whole process again.

Handwriting

The handwriting test will consist of another piece of writing to be copied, perhaps a continuation of the story used for the spelling exercise. The test should occupy about five minutes.

Study item: handwriting

Write out this part of the *Snow White* story, joining the letters if you can, making your writing as neat as you can.

Snow White ran away into a great forest. Her step-mother the queen sent someone to kill her, but the girl came across a little house occupied by seven dwarfs. The dwarfs looked after the girl until a prince came along and fell in love with her and married her.

What the examiners will be looking for

At Level 5 the examiners will expect to see an attractive, joined, flowing type of writing which is neat and easy to read.

In order to attain the average Level 4 grading, the child will have to produce a style of handwriting which is clear and legible, with regular-sized spacing and sizing. This writing should show the child's ability to join letters together.

Below this level, handwriting will be graded at Levels 3, 2 and 1, depending upon the standard shown. At Level 1, the child only has to show the ability to write some recognisable letters.

Studying the handwriting test at home

What the examiners are looking for is a neat, well-controlled form of handwriting, using joined letters. Your child will be getting plenty of practice in this at school. You can best help by checking for general neatness and legibility whenever she does any writing at home.

ENGLISH TEST PAPER – KEY STAGE 2

Read this story and then answer the questions on it.

Time: 40 minutes

The Geese Who Kept Guard

More than two thousand years ago the people of Rome sent their soldiers away to fight in a war. This was a brave but foolish act. It left no one to guard the city. The general in charge of the army always obeyed orders and took the army away from the city. The enemies of Rome, who were called the Gauls, decided to attack Rome. The people of Rome fought bravely, but without trained soldiers to help them they were forced inside the city walls. The Gauls waited outside to attack. One night they found a secret path into the city and crept along it. None of the Roman sentries saw them. The Gauls passed a large area where many geese

were kept to be sacrificed to the gods.
The geese heard the Gauls and began
to honk loudly. This awoke the citizens
of Rome, who got up and drove the
Gauls away. The Roman army returned
soon afterwards and the Gauls marched
away. To reward the geese who saved
Rome it was decided that never again
would one of these birds be sacrificed to
the gods.

1 This story took place
  last week   100 years ago   more than
  500 years ago   more than 2000 years
  ago
2 The Roman soldiers went away
  to fight in a war   to go on holiday
  because they did not like Rome   to
  build a new city
3 The enemies who attacked Rome were
  the French   the English   the Gauls
  the Germans
4 The geese were kept by the Romans
  as Christmas presents   to start a zoo
  to sacrifice to the Gods   to supply eggs
5 When the geese heard the Gauls they
  laid a lot of eggs   ran away   started
  honking   did nothing
6 To reward the geese the Romans
  gave them gold   stopped sacrificing
  them to the Gods   improved their
  homes   let them go
7 Find the words in the story which say

why the Romans had to retreat behind the city walls.

8 How did the Romans feel about the geese after the Gauls had been driven away?

bored   hungry   grateful   depressed

9 Write down another suitable title for this story.

10 When they were disturbed the geese *honked* loudly. Think of two other words you could use in place of *honked*.

11 Which two adjectives at the beginning of the story describe the action of the citizens in sending their soldiers away to fight in a war?

12 When the Roman general was ordered to take his army away his response to the order tells us something about him. What sort of man do you think he was?

Time: 40 minutes

The Death of Nelson

In 1805, the British won the great naval battle at Trafalgar. In the middle of the battle the British admiral Lord Nelson on board his vessel the *Victory* was shot by a French sniper, firing from the French ship *Redoubtable*. As he fell Nelson cried, ''They have done for me, my backbone is shot through!'' Some of Nelson's sailors carried their admiral tenderly below. As he was carried down Nelson covered his face with his handkerchief, so that the

ENGLISH TESTS FOR TEN- AND ELEVEN-YEAR-OLDS

fighting men would not see his condition
and be dismayed. He was examined by the
surgeon and given lemonade to quench
his thirst, but little could be done for him.
He died soon afterwards.

1 Where was the great naval battle
fought?
Waterloo   Agincourt   Trafalgar   Cairo
2 In which year was it fought?
1205   1805   1605   1995
3 Which were the two countries fighting in
the battle?
Britain and France   America and Japan
Germany and Ireland   Holland and
Belgium
4 Which two ships are mentioned in the
story?
Armada   Victory   Redoubtable   Great
Harry
5 Who shot Lord Nelson?
a madman   a grenadier   a French
sniper   a spy
6 Why did Nelson cover his face with a
handkerchief?
because he was tired   because he did
not want to see anyone   so that his men
would not see his condition
7 What words in the story tell us that
Nelson knew he was going to die?
'I am dying!'   'Goodbye!'   'They have
shot me!'   'They have done for me!'
8 While the sailors were carrying Lord

Nelson below, which word in the
sentence beginning 'Some of Nelson's
sailors ...' tells us that they cared
greatly for the admiral.
sorrowfully   tenderly   sadly   quickly

Time: 30 minutes

Trees

The oak is called the king of trees,
The aspen quivers in the breeze,
The poplar grows up straight and tall,
The pear tree spreads along the wall,
The sycamore gives pleasant shade,
The willow droops in watery glade,
The fir tree useful timber gives,
The beech amid the forest lives.

Sara Coleridge

1 This poem is about
  the countryside   weather   trees
  water
2 How many trees does the poem mention?
  5   8   7   6
3 What does the word *quivers* means in
  the line '*The aspen quivers in the
  breeze*'?
4 What does the word *droops* mean in
  the line '*The willow droops in watery
  glade*'?
5 What does it mean when it says that
  the pear tree *spreads* along the wall?
6 What does it mean when it says that
  the oak is the *king* of trees?

7 What sort of useful timber do you think the fir gives?
8 Which tree gives a pleasant shade?
9 Which tree grows in a watery glade?
10 What is a watery glade?

Time: 40 minutes

Story Writing

Write a story using the starting points given below. Before you start writing the story spend some time planning it. Give your story a title. Make sure that it is about life-like characters. Give the story a dramatic beginning. Plan an exciting ending for the story. Lead up to this ending with an interesting story.

- You are in a spaceship.
- You have two friends with you.
- You are about to land on an unknown planet.
- You can only stay on the planet for ten minutes.
- Then you must start the long flight home.

Time: 40 minutes

Letter Writing

Write a letter to a pop-star or television star asking him or her to come to your school and present prizes at an end-of-term meeting. Tell the star why you admire him or her. Try to think of a reason which might persuade the star to come to your school.

- Start the letter with the school's address and the date.
- Tell the star why you like him or her.
- Tell the star what you want him or her to do.
- Give a good reason or some good reasons for the star to come to your school.

Time: 30 minutes

Handwriting and Spelling

Copy out this story in your best joined handwriting. Spell each of the words in the spaces.

The farmer and his sons

An old farmer was very ill. He knew that he was going to d_____. He had three sons. He called each of his b_____ to his death bed. 'I will s_____ be d_____,' he s_____. 'I have dug deep down into the earth and b_____ some gold on the f_____. The first of y_____ to dig it up may k_____ it.' The farmer died. His three sons dug all the s_____ on the farm. They f_____ no gold, but they had dug the e_____ so well that it gave great crops. That was j_____ what the old farmer had m_____ to h_____.

Test answers

Reading comprehension

The geese who kept guard
1 More than 2000 years ago.
2 To fight in a war.
3 The Gauls
4 To sacrifice to the gods.
5 Started honking
6 Stopped sacrificing them to the gods.
7 'Without trained soldiers to help them.'
8 Grateful
9 Give one mark for anything about the geese saving Rome.
10 Give credit for any suitable words meaning making a loud noise – cackled, etc.
11 Brave, foolish
12 Give a mark for any word meaning loyal, well disciplined, etc.
(Total: 12)

The death of Nelson
1 Trafalgar
2 1805
3 Britain and France
4 Victory, Redoubtable
5 A French sniper
6 So that his men would not see his condition.
7 'They have done for me!'
8 Tenderly
(Total: 8)

Trees
1 Trees
2 8
3 Anything that means shivers or shakes.
4 Anything that means hangs or bends.

5 Anything that means stretches or extends or reaches.
6 It is the best tree.
7 For making houses, furniture, etc.
8 Sycamore
9 Willow
10 An open space amid trees, with a stream or similar source of water.

(Total: 10)

Writing – story

If you wish to attempt to assess your child's creative writing exercise, the following marks scheme out of 20 may be of use.

Contents	Range of marks
A good basic story, starting well and going on to a satisfactory ending. Good use of sentences.	5–10
A lively story with an organised beginning, middle and end, with good use of vocabulary, sentences and paragraphs. Dialogue is presented between speech marks. The title is relevant and interesting. The characters are well defined.	10–15
An imaginative, well-organised story ending in an exciting climax. The characters contrast well with one another. There is a theme as well as a plot. Full stops, commas, capital letters, question marks, are all used with confidence. The title should attract interest.	15–20

Writing – letter

A possible subjective marking scheme out of 20 which could be used while assessing the letter is provided below.

Contents	Range of marks
A reasonably well set out letter, with the heading in the right place. Somewhere in the letter the intention for writing may be discerned. The handwriting is reasonably clear. There are quite a few spelling and grammatical errors.	5–10
A clear, logical, if not very interesting letter, well set out, in which the objective is made clear somewhere in the contents. The handwriting is clear and there are only a few errors of grammar and spelling.	10–15
An interesting, well-planned letter, with the heading correctly set out. The reason for writing the letter is set out in the opening sentences. The letter develops in a logical and pleasant manner and ends in a suitable way. The handwriting is clear and there are no grammatical or spelling mistakes. Something of the personality of the writer may be detected.	15–20

Spelling

1 Die

2 Boys

3 Soon

4 Dead

5 Said
6 Buried
7 Farm
8 You
9 Keep
10 Soil
11 Found
12 Earth
13 Just
14 Meant
15 Happen
(Total: 15)

Handwriting

A subjective marking scheme out of 10 could be:

Style	Range of marks
Not joined, letters of different sizes, generally untidy.	0–2
Not joined, letters of same sizes, generally tidy.	2–4
Joined, generally untidy.	4–6
Joined, tidy.	6–8
Joined, tidy, attractive, with a distinctive style.	9–10

Gradings

Give one mark for each correct answer in the reading and spelling tests, and give an appropriate score from the grading columns for handwriting, story writing and letter writing.

ENGLISH TESTS FOR TEN- AND ELEVEN-YEAR-OLDS

Ratings for reading comprehension

Marks	Level	Rating
22–30	5	above average
12–21	4	average
0–11	3	below average

Ratings for writing

Marks	Level	Rating
30–40	5	above average
16–29	4	average
0–15	3	below average

Ratings for spelling

Marks	Level	Rating
11–15	5	above average
8–10	4	average
0–7	3	below average

Ratings for handwriting

Marks	Level	Rating
8–10	5	above average
4–7	4	average
0–3	3	below average

Overall English ratings

Marks	Level	Rating
70–95	5	above average
38–69	4	average
0–37	3 (or below)	below average

Parents talking

❝ In an effort to get my son interested in reading I took him along to the Public Library. He took one look at the rows of shelves and said in the most doleful of tones, "It's just a load of books!" Somehow I don't think he's quite ready for independent reading yet! ❞

❝ I wanted to help my twins at home with the English test, but as soon as I saw the curriculum I knew I was on a loser. They could cope with the talking part, no bother, but synchronised listening was well beyond them! ❞

Useful books at Key Stage 2

Parents

The Parents' Guide to National Tests – Key Stage 2 English, HMSO.

Prepare Your Child for Key Stage 2 National Tests English, John Lisle, Letts.

Children

Spotlight on the English Language, Sandy Brownjohn and Gareth Gwyn-Jones, Hodder and Stoughton.

Stories for Thinking, Robert Fisher, Nash Pollock.

Primary School Tests and Quizzes, Graeme Kent, Pearson.

Assessment Papers in English – 10–11 years, J. M. Bond, Nelson.

Oxford Primary English, Books 3 and 4, Bernadette Fitzgerald, Kay Hiatt, Joyce Hilyer, O.U.P.

CHAPTER SIX

Mathematics tests for ten- and eleven-year-olds

Maths

I would like schools lots and lots,
It's just over Maths I get tied in knots.
Science is easy, English is quick,
Art is over in a very short tick.
But Maths I loathe – struggling along –
How many? How much? Oh dear, I've gone wrong!
Divisions, tables, adding and take
Add this, take that – how much does this make?
Two sevens, five fours and six threes,
Seventy-four people – how many knees?
Fractions and signs, and all those numbers –
Sixty-seven pipes, how many plumbers?
I would like school lots and lots.
It's just over Maths I get tied in knots.

Claire, aged ten

When your child reaches the age of eleven he will take two mathematics test papers. He will also be tested in mental arithmetic. These papers should decide whether your child has reached Levels 3, 4 or 5. The average child of this age is expected to attain Level

4. If your child's teacher regards him as being particularly gifted in this subject he will be given an extra paper, which will give him a chance to reach the even higher Level 6.

Children will be tested in the aspects of mathematics they have covered in the National Curriculum in the junior school – number, shape, space and measures, handling data. These branches of mathematics will be taught both individually and as parts of combined projects in the classroom. Your child will be expected to use and apply all these types of mathematics in a variety of tests and situations.

Using and applying mathematics

There will be a number of questions in the tests designed to see how well your child can adapt his theoretical knowledge of mathematics and use it in certain contexts. The examiners want to see if he can apply his knowledge to real-life situations, select the right methods to solve problems and use the language of mathematics appropriately. This last requirement may range from knowing the meaning of simple words like *add* and *take*, to more complex concepts like *probability*.

Your child will be presented with a number of practical problems which can be solved if he selects the right mathematical tools and applies them correctly.

What the examiners will be looking for

The questions will be designed to show how your child approaches the problem given him, how he selects the correct techniques and adapts them to the particular needs of the project, discarding methods which do not work, and how he devises and refines ways of recording the working and the answers.

To reach the average grading of Level 4 a child will show a reasonable ability to apply what he has learnt to the solving of real-life mathematical problems, but probably will not consider as many possible approaches as a more gifted child, and will not present his working and solutions in such a polished manner.

A child graded at Level 5 should be able to collect and use essential information, check results, and describe situations using the appropriate words, diagrams and symbols.

A child who can accomplish all this, in conjunction with the other strands of the mathematics curriculum, will probably be considered above average at the use and application of mathematics and will be given additional problems to solve to see if he can maintain this level of reasoning and reach Level 6. The standards necessary for a Level 6 grading will be found in Chapter 9.

Studying the use and application of mathematics at home

Let your child see you using and applying mathematics to everyday tasks about the home. If you are weighing amounts for cooking, measuring a space before fitting a piece of furniture into it, working out the number of stamps you need to put on a parcel before posting it, involve your child in the calculations and let him see how important and integral a knowledge of practical mathematics is in your everyday life.

Encourage him to participate in activities around the house which involve selecting and applying the right sort of mathematical techniques.

Study item: counting, measuring, estimating

- Play board games which involve calculating and counting.
- Estimate, compare and check the weights of different objects – is this book heavier than that clock?
- Estimate and check fractions of distances – how far is it halfway across the living room?
- Identify basic shapes in common objects – that mat is round, this screen is square, etc.

The language of mathematics

Implicit in all the test questions will be the assumption that your child understands the basic language of mathematics and can understand the terms and phraseology of the questions. Some examples of mathematical language occur frequently in the tests at Key Stage 2. These concepts are dealt with below and throughout the chapter.

What the examiners are looking for

Children will be expected to understand quickly what is expected of them when they read the questions and to be able to set about finding straight away the best ways to answer the questions, without being bogged down in puzzling out the meaning of the mathematical terms and concepts used in the test papers. The longer it takes your child to work out what is wanted of him, the less time he will have to complete all the questions set. No special marks will be given for your child's ability to distinguish what is required, but it is essential that he understands the basic language of mathematics needed at this stage of his school life.

Studying the language of mathematics at home

Using the basic terms of mathematics aloud as you work about the house will reinforce your child's understanding of mathematical language. He will become accustomed to hearing such terms as *half of, divide, multiply, measure, estimate,* and so on.

There are a number of important terms used in the tests at Key Stage 2, which are often tested. You can help your child and familiarise him with their meaning by talking to him about them and showing him examples of how they may be applied to everyday situations. At this stage it is particularly important that your child knows the meanings of the following words and concepts. Give him regular exercises in the use and application of the different terms.

Study item: mathematical terms

- **Angles:** An angle is the space between two lines or surfaces that meet or cross each other.
- **Degrees:** Angles are measured in *degrees*. Particular kinds of angles which children should know about at this stage are *right angles*, which measure 90 degrees, *obtuse angles*, which measure between 90 degrees and 180 degrees, and *acute angles*, which measure less than 90 degrees. Help your child by drawing a number of angles and asking him to measure them with a protractor and say what sort of angle each one is.
- **Attributes:** An attribute is a quality belonging to something. In mathematical terms at this level it usually means a quality of an *attribute block*. These qualities are *size, colour, thickness* and *shape*. Get hold of some ordinary wooden and plastic shapes and make sure that your child can sub-divide them by their size, colour, thickness and shape.
- **Area:** The area of an object is the size of its surface. This is found by multiplying its length by its width. Ask your child to estimate or guess the area of a table-top, floor, etc, and then check it by measuring the length and the width and multiplying the two measurements.
- **Capacity:** The capacity of an object is the amount it can hold. Help your child by giving him a litre measuring jug and asking him to estimate how much water different containers will hold. He should check the estimate by pouring water from the measuring jug into the different containers.
- **Diagrams:** A diagram is a plan or a figure drawn to explain an idea. Diagrams which children may draw at home can include ones to illustrate the temperatures over a period of time, weather recording, etc.
- **Graphs:** A basic graph is a straight or curved line drawn between a vertical line and a horizontal line across the page to show how the two lines of information, represented horizontally and vertically, are related to one another, for

example how much rain falls each month over a period of a year. Other graphs which children are expected to understand at Key Stage 2 are *block graphs,* where individual squares are coloured in to represent data, and *bar graphs,* in which whole columns are drawn to provide information. A *pie graph* is a circle divided into sections, each section representing a different part of the whole circle. Ask your child to use line, block, bar and pie graphs to show such things as the number of sunny days in a month, the favourite foods of the children in his class, and so on.

- **Grids:** A grid is a set of squares, each one the same size, formed by intersecting straight lines. In the tests children are sometimes asked to draw geometrical shapes like rectangles or triangles, of varying sizes, on a grid provided. Give your child practice in drawing shapes on a grid – a triangle covering six squares, etc.

- **Probability:** Children must gain experience in deciding whether, given certain facts, the outcome is *possible, likely* or *probable.*

- **Tesselation:** Tesselation is the name given to a pattern in which shapes fit exactly, without overlapping or leaving gaps. Give your child practice in using coloured sticky paper of different shapes to make tesselated patterns.

Number

By Year 6, when your child will be taking the Key Stage 2 tests, he will be expected to know a number of basic mathematical facts and techniques and be able to answer questions involving the use of what has been learned.

What the examiners will be looking for

Your child will be expected to answer a number of basic mechanical mathematical questions and to use his knowledge of skills and techniques to understand what is required of him in more complex mathematical situations. To achieve the average grading of Level 4, your child should be comfortable with the use of figures and basic skills in a number of contexts.

In order to be graded at the above average of Level 5 your child should also be able to demonstrate an ability to cope with more difficult aspects of the curriculum, finding fractions and decimals of wholes, applying the four rules to fractions and decimals, dealing with large numbers.

An above average child, rated at Level 5, will be allowed to go on and take an extra paper to see if he is working at Level 6.

Studying number at home

Many of the number activities to be found in the test papers at Key Stage 2 may be prepared for with the use of a calculator at home. These will help him cope with the number questions set at Key Stage 2.

Study item: calculator activities

- Go through the tables up to 10×10, and check answers with a calculator.
- Use a calculator to solve answers to problems.
- Check the answers to mental arithmetic activities.
- Keep a record of the number of people met in a day.
- Play dice games, recording scores.
- Play games using any two numbers at a time (e.g. 5 and 3). How many numbers can be made by using all the arithmetical signs on the calculator and applying them to the two chosen numbers?
- Apply the four rules to weight, time, money, length, etc and check the answers with a calculator.
- Change common fractions to decimal fractions, i.e. $\frac{1}{2} = 1$ divided by $2 = 0.5$, etc.

It will help your child greatly if you also help him with inserting missing numbers or signs in sums, as this aspect of number is often tested at this level.

Study item: missing numbers

- Practise working out sums which have a missing number, e.g.

$$
\begin{array}{r}
46 \\
5*+ \\
18 \\
\hline
118
\end{array}
$$

- The point of this question is to work out which digit should take the place of the asterisk in order to complete the sum. It is an aspect of number work which can soon become second nature to the child if he is just given practice at home. All that you need to do is to work out the complete sum, e.g.

$$
\begin{array}{r}
46 \\
24- \\
\hline
22
\end{array}
$$

Before you give it to your child, take out one of the digits and replace it with a dash or an asterisk.

$$
\begin{array}{r}
4* \\
24 \ - \\
\hline
22
\end{array}
$$

- Sometimes the test question will ask your child to put in the correct mathematical sign, i.e. addition, subtraction, division or multiplication. You can give your child examples of these at home as well: 42 ? 2 $\times$ 21;   8 ? 4 = 32;   12 ? 8 = 20.

Shape, space and measures

Children will be tested on their knowledge and understanding of geometrical shapes, patterns, position, movement and measurement.

What the examiners will be looking for

The examiners will expect the average child at Key Stage 4 to compare and differentiate between different shapes which have parallel sides, etc, to be able to draw lines of symmetry, to draw angles, work out areas, use charts and diagrams, and draw reflections of objects.

Children of above average ability – those at Level 5 or working towards Level 6 – will be expected to cover the work undertaken at Level 4 and go on to demonstrate more intricate skills and techniques, including how to understand probability, place numbers in patterns of increasing difficulty, estimate and approximate from information given, work out sequences, interpret and draw graphs.

Studying shape, space and measures at home

The most effective ways of helping your child prepare for the questions on shape, space and measures which he might be given in the tests at Key Stage 2 will be to help him recognise and draw shapes and patterns, understand and use the properties of position and movement, and understand and use measures.

Study item: shapes and patterns

- Study and draw isosceles triangles (triangles with two equal sides).
- Study and draw equilateral triangles (triangles with three equal sides).
- Use squared paper to show that different shapes have the same areas.
- Examine three-dimensional solids in order to understand that 3D means having three dimensions or attributes – length, breadth and height. Measure the length and breadth and height of 3D shapes.
- Practise drawing to scale on squared paper. Use a scale of one square to represent something – a metre, ten metres, etc.

- See how many different shapes can be made by using twelve matchboxes in various combinations. Do this with real matchboxes and then make pictorial representations of what has been done.

Study item: position and movement

- Examine *rigid* and *non-rigid* shapes. Make shapes out of pliable materials. See what happens when they are pushed and pulled. Represent these movements in a series of pictures.
- Use toy cars and push them along a surface, making a series of right-angled turns. Record these turns in a sequence of pictures.
- Examine the number of connecting shapes about the house. Say whether each one is greater or smaller than a right angle.
- Use a compass to mark out the directions to take in and around the house to reach different locations. Make pictorial representations of these routes.

Handling data

The test papers will ask your child to analyse information which is provided for him and to draw conclusions from his interpretations of this information. He will be asked to understand and handle simple statistics and interpret data.

What the examiners will be looking for

The questions will be designed to ensure that your child can approach sources of information in an unflustered manner, extract from this information what is needed and then use the information to provide an answer to the question.

As long as a child is given enough practice in handling and using data on a regular basis, he should have few problems when he is faced with these sorts of questions.

An average child should be able to use timetables and brochures, undertake surveys, solve simple crossword and jigsaw puzzles, put together simple constructional toys from the leaflets provided, use a calendar, make out and check bills and receipts, enter and access simple information on a computer database, prepare meals from recipes and interpret simple plans. The ability to cope with this sort of data would be enough for a grading at Level 4.

Those children who can also devise 'fair' and 'unfair' tests, predict with accuracy the outcome of situations based on information provided, use conversion charts, study and record the information provided on dials, meters, etc, devise games and work out methods of scoring, will be graded at Level 5 and allowed to take the extra paper to see if they can reach Level 6.

Children with difficulty in handling data and whose efforts are mainly confined to telling the time, retrieving information from simple pamphlets and programmes, and so on, would probably be rated at Level 3. Handling data is not covered at Key Stage 1.

Studying handling data at home

This is one of the most important, yet also one of the easiest, ways in which you can help your child prepare for the mathematics test at home. So much of our daily life is governed by data which we have to interpret and act upon that it is not difficult to include children in examining and acting upon different sorts of information provided.

Encourage your child to read catalogues and add up the total cost of purchases he would like to make. Ask him to work out arrival and departure times from bus and train timetables. Read and record the daily temperature from a thermometer. Work out who is playing in different positions recorded in a football programme. Make a study of local post-codes and find out what they mean.

There are also more specific activities which your child can undertake at home which will prepare him for the sorts of questions he will face in the tests at Key Stage 2.

HELP YOUR CHILD WITH THE NATIONAL CURRICULUM TESTS

Study item: data handling activities

- Play a game with a die. Make a record sheet with a line for each of the six numbers on the die. Then roll the die 25 times. Place a cross against each number on the record sheet as the die is rolled. Is it possible to guess what number will be rolled the 26th time? Think about this.
- Distinguish between 'fair' and 'unfair' tests. Play a game of snakes and ladders with a parent. You only have one die to roll, but your parent has two dice to roll at the same time. Is this a fair or an unfair game?
- Put five events in each of these columns about your everyday life:

  Things which   *Things which*   *Things which*
  are sure to happen   *may happen*   *probably will*
                                              not happen

- Carry out an exercise in probability. Take a pack of 52 playing cards. What is the probability of getting the King of Clubs every time a card is dealt to you? Work this out in theory and then devise a practical experiment with the cards, recording the results.

MATHEMATICS TEST PAPER – KEY STAGE 2

Number

Time: 40 minutes

Divide the following numbers by 100.
Some answers will have remainders

| 1 4520 | 2 6580 | 3 980 | 4 120 | 5 650 |
| 6 3478 | 7 5998 | 8 2491 | 9 4893 | 10 8759 |

Add these sums.

11 56	12 63	13 75	14 57	15 32
46	32	12	45	18
+19	+21	+36	+15	+49
——	——	——	——	——

Subtract these sums.

16	46	**17**	38	**18**	57	**19**	63	**20**	78
	-35		-17		-45		-32		-45

Multiply these sums.

21	32	**22**	12	**23**	15	**24**	14	**25**	16
	$\times\ 4$		$\times\ 3$		$\times\ 4$		$\times\ 5$		$\times\ 6$

Estimate these answers and then check them with a calculator:

	Estimate	**Calculator**
26 11×12		
27 20×10		
28 50×3		
29 60×4		
30 45×6		
31 80×20		

Using mathematics

Time: 20 minutes

These fans supported their football team on four Saturday games:

Game 1:	**Game 2:**	**Game 3:**	**Game 4:**
5543	4689	3568	3456

1 How many people attended the four games?

2 Which game had the most supporters?

3 Which game had the least attenders?

4 How many more people saw the first
game than saw the second game?
5 What was the average (mean)
attendance for the four games?

Shape, space and measures

Time: 20 minutes
Measure and mark the half-way point on
these three lines:

1 _____
2 _____
3 _____

Mark the following directions on this
compass:

4 West
5 North-east
6 East
7 South-west
8 South-east
9 North-west

Handling data

Time: 20 minutes
1 Draw a graph showing the monthly
rainfall over a six-month period.
January: 5 cm   February: 10 cm
March: 30 cm   April: 10 cm
May: 20 cm   June: 5 cm

Calendar for February

Sun.	Mon.	Tues.	Weds.	Thurs.	Fri.	Sat.
				1	2	3
4	5	6	7	8	9	10
11	12	13	14	15	16	17
18	19	20	21	22	23	24
25	26	27	28			

On which days of the week do these dates fall?

2 8th   **3** 13th   **4** 18th   **5** 5th

Test answers

Number

1 45 r 20	**2** 65 r 80	**3** 9 r 80	**4** l r 20	**5** 6 r 50
6 34 r 78	**7** 59 r 98	**8** 24 r 91	**9** 48 r 93	**10** 87 r 59
11 121	**12** 116	**13** 123	**14** 117	**15** 99
16 11	**17** 21	**18** 12	**19** 31	**20** 33
21 128	**22** 36	**23** 60	**24** 70	**25** 96

Calculator activities (26–31). Give half a mark if the calculation is right and another half if the estimate is within 20 of the calculator results. In the answers below the calculator result is placed second.

26 * 132   **27** * 200   **28** * 150   **29** * 240
30 * 270   **31** * 1600
(Total 31)

Using mathematics

1 17256   **2** Game 1   **3** Game 4   **4** 854   **5** 4314
(Total: 5)

Shape, space and measures

1 42 mm **2** 33 mm **3** 37 mm

4–9

(Total: 9)

Handling data

1

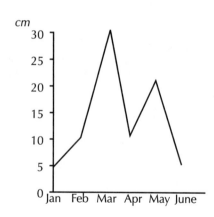

2 Thursday
3 Tuesday
4 Sunday
5 Monday
(Total: 5)

Gradings

Number

Marks	Level	Rating
24–31	5	above average
14–23	4	average
0–13	3	below average

Using mathematics

Marks	Level	Rating
4–5	5	above average
3–4	4	average
0–2	3	below average

Shape, space and measures

Marks	Level	Rating
7–9	5	above average
4–6	4	average
0–3	3	below average

Handling data

Marks	Level	Rating
4–5	5	above average
3–4	4	average
0–2	3	below average

Overall mathematics ratings

Marks	Level	Rating
38–50	5	above average
22–37	4	average
0–21	3 (or below)	below average

Parents talking

❝ *I thought I was beginning to break through in mathematics when my son was able to tell me that geometry was 'them things with corners'.* ❞

❝ *I realised how much things had changed since I was a child when I was working out some bus timetables with my daughter for homework and she asked me what a bus was.* ❞

Useful books at Key Stage 2

Parents

Lines of development in primary mathematics, Mary Deboys and Eunice Pitt, Blackstaff Press.
The Parents' Guide to National Tests Mathematics, HMSO.

Children

Investigating Areas, Ed Catherall, Wayland.
Investigating Graphs, Ed Catherall, Wayland.
Investigating Angles, Ed Catherall, Wayland.
Statistics, R. Russell, Watts.
Key Number Skills, Norman D. Lock, Ladybird.
Leap Ahead With Maths series, Brian Nash and Paul Nightingale, Nightingale Press.
Assessment Papers in Mathematics – 10–11 years, J. M. Bond, Nelson.

CHAPTER SEVEN

Science tests for ten- and eleven-year-olds

> *Inside the Gravity Wheel at the Fair*
> *The gravity wheel is always busy.*
> *Round and round, it makes you dizzy!*
> *You're stuck inside this dreadful thing.*
> *You can't get out, or dance or sing.*
> *You learn in Science that gravity's good.*
> *I don't think that from where I'm stood!*
>
> *Carly, aged 9*

In Year 6 your child will take two science test papers. There will be about ten questions in each test. The two papers will cover the three main strands of science – *Life Processes and Living Things*, *Materials and their Properties* and *Physical Processes*. Children will also be expected to demonstrate an ability to handle experimental and investigative science.

Each test will last 35 minutes. The average child should attain Level 4, and the above average child should reach Level 5. Those children judged by their teacher capable of reaching Level 6 will be given an extra 30-minute test. Those children who are considered to be below average at this stage will be graded at Levels 3, 2 or 1. The standards for these levels are given in Chapter 4. If the teacher believes that a child will only attain Levels 1 or 2 then the child will not have to do the tests at Key Stage 2. The standards for Levels 6, 7 and 8 may be found in Chapter 10.

Experimental and investigative science

Throughout the tests the examiners will be trying to find out how well your child can apply what she has learnt to various scientific problems. She will be expected to measure and to carry out experiments.

What the examiners will be looking for

A child of average ability, capable of reaching Level 4, should be able to recognise the need for fair tests, select suitable equipment, make predictions, present observations using charts, graphs and diagrams, recognise patterns, draw conclusions and begin to relate these conclusions to scientific knowledge and understanding.

Children rated at Level 5 should be able to do all these things and also to say what the important points are in any findings, repeat experiments and be able to account for any differences they encounter when doing so.

Studying investigative and experimental science at home

Encourage your child to take an interest in all aspects of science and technology about the house, at the same time making sure that she is always supervised when carrying out any investigations. Answer her questions about the sources of heat and lighting, the purpose of various aspects of technology in the kitchen, and so on.

Study item: investigations

- Test the strength of cardboard pillars. Make a number of cardboard pillars of different sizes, sticking them into position with tape. Stand each one upright, with a piece of cardboard across the top. Predict which one should be the strongest.

SCIENCE TESTS FOR TEN- AND ELEVEN-YEAR-OLDS

Think of a way of testing the strength of each pillar. How much weight will each support before it collapses. Which one was the strongest?

- Test the power of different magnets. Collect a number of magnets of different shapes and sizes. Predict which one should attract the most filings. Devise a fair test. Write about what happens. Illustrate your answer with diagrams
- Make a collection of different plants. Take them to pieces. Name the component parts of each one – stems, roots, leaves, etc. State what each part does in the plant. Compare the same parts of the different plants. Write about the similarities and differences and illustrate your answers
- Find out what the word *lubrication* means. Make a list of things which can be lubricated to move more easily. What happens when moving parts are not lubricated?

There are a number of basic words and phrases connected with scientific investigation which the examiners will expect your child to understand. Over a period make sure that she is familiar with most of them and knows how to apply them.

Key facts to learn

- **Data:** Facts or information.
- **Evidence:** Words which prove a statement.
- **Fair test:** A test which gives all the elements in an experiment or investigation the same chance.
- **Hypothesis:** A basic idea which might explain the facts.
- **Key factors:** The most important results of an investigation.
- **Prediction:** To describe in advance what might happen or ought to happen.

Life Processes and Living Things

These questions will be concerned mainly with humans and plants. At Level 4 the average child should be able to give the scientific names of some of the major organs and systems of the human body and know where they are. Similarly, she should be able to name and identify some of the parts of plants. She will be expected to recognise and describe how animals and plants feed and take in nourishment.

What the examiners will be looking for

The examiners will be looking for signs that your child knows about mammals and plants and different life processes – breathing, digestion, circulation of blood, etc. She should also know about aspects of good health in humans. She will be expected to understand the main similarities and differences between humans, plants, animals and non-living objects like rocks. If she can show signs of understanding these areas she should attain an average rating of Level 4.

To reach the above average rating of Level 5, children will also be expected to demonstrate an increasing knowledge and understanding of life processes and living things. These will include describing the main functions of some organs of the human body and explaining the importance of these functions. They should also be able to describe and compare the life cycles of humans and flowering plants, as well as to classify living things and understand the importance of the environment to humans and plants.

Studying life and living processes at home

It is important that you make sure that your child knows about the main organs of the human body – heart, lungs, liver, etc and what their functions are. Similarly, it will be a great help if you can check that your child understands about the different parts of plants – stems, leaves, roots, and so on – and how they contribute to the life of the plant. If you can use diagrams of the human body and of plants, and question your child about the main parts of each, this will be of considerable use to her in the tests.

Study item: life and living processes

- Make a chart with two headings: *Living things* and *Non-living things*. Apply these tests as to whether something is living. Does it grow? Does it reproduce? Does it take in food? Does it give off waste? Can it move? Can it sense? A *yes* answer to any of these means that the object is living.
- Keep a record of your own physical measurements and update it every six months. Use these headings: *Height, Weight, Chest, Waist, Length of foot, Span of hand, Neck.*
- Conduct an experiment to show how the muscles of the stomach squeeze food through the digestive tract. Squeeze a marble through a tube from one end to the other. Write about this experiment, saying what it has shown. Draw diagrams to illustrate the report.

Key facts to learn about plants

- **Roots:** Hold a plant in the ground and take in water which contain salts, helping the plant to grow.
- **Stem:** Water and salts flow through the stem from the roots to the rest of the plant.
- **Leaves:** These are attached to the stem. The sun builds up sugar in the leaves to feed the plant.
- **Flowers:** In most plants, seeds develop in the flowers. From these seeds fresh plants grow.

Key facts to learn about the human body

- **Blood:** The red liquid which flows round the body.
- **Heart:** Controls the flow of blood through the body by pumping it.
- **Kidneys:** A pair of organs which separate waste liquid from the blood to pass it from the body.
- **Lungs:** The breathing organs in the chest, taking in fresh air and expelling stale air.
- **Muscles:** Collections of fibres which enable the body to move.

- **Skeleton:** The bones of the body, which protect the organs.
- **Stomach:** An organ in the body which digests food or breaks it down for use in the body.

Materials and their properties

The questions in this section of the tests will be concerned at a fairly basic level with chemistry. Children will be expected to place things in different groups, and know how and why some things change. At Level 4, the child rated as being of average ability will be expected to know that some materials are natural (rocks) and others are man-made (plastic). She should understand that materials differ in their textures and be able to describe the differences between the properties of these different materials. In particular she should be able to understand the differences between solids, liquids and gases. She should be able to explain how methods like filtration are used to separate simple mixtures. She should be able to use such terms as *condensation* or *evaporation* to describe changes. She should be able to predict whether some changes are reversible or not.

What the examiners will be looking for

To be graded at Level 4, the examiners will expect your child to have a good understanding of the materials in the world around her, both natural and man-made. She should be able to find and explain similarities and differences between these materials. She should know about some of the properties of materials, e.g. their shapes, colours, degrees of hardness or softness. The examiners will expect her to know the differences between solids, liquids and gases and how these may be changed from one state to another. The concept of change is also an important one at this stage.

To reach Level 5 a child will also be expected to describe aspects of rocks and metals, such as metals which conduct electricity effectively, and use these properties to distinguish metals from other solids. She should be able to identify a range of contexts in which changes such as evaporation or condensation take place. She should use knowledge about how specific mixtures, such as salt and water, or sand and water can be separated to suggest ways in which other similar mixtures might be separated.

Studying materials and their properties at home

Give your child opportunities to handle many different materials, weighing them, assessing them for strength, deciding whether they are hard or soft. Make sure that she can recognise and describe solids, liquids and gases and can place materials in one of these three categories. Give her opportunities to take part in activities which involve change, i.e. making jelly, dough, and so on. It will also help if you can show her examples of weathering in the locality and make sure that she understands that buildings, rocks, trees, etc., have changed in shape or size because of the effects of weather.

Study item: materials and their properties

- Make a small wall out of concrete. Mix together some sand, gravel and cement. Use just enough water to bind these ingredients together. Make the wet concrete in the shape of a wall and leave it to dry. Devise some tests to see how strong it is
- Examine the properties of twenty different materials. Put them under the headings *Objects which bend* and *Objects which do not bend*. Think of other properties for which you could test the same materials
- Conduct a number of experiments and see how many things you can find which will dissolve in water
- Collect twenty different objects. Conduct experiments and put each one under one of these headings: *Objects which float* and *Objects which do not float*
- Draw a diagram to show that you understand the theory of the

water cycle. (Water falls to Earth as rain. It lies there in rivers, lakes, the sea, etc. The heat of the Sun causes the water to evaporate and rise. As it rises it cools, forms into clouds and falls to Earth as rain again.)

Key facts to learn about materials

- **Chemical change:** This comes about when an entirely new substance is made through the action of one substance on another, i.e. a mixture of metal and oxygen can cause rust.
- **Elements:** Everything around us is made up of substances or chemicals. An element is a simple substance which is not mixed with anything else, e.g. iron, gold, etc.
- **Compounds:** Anything that is not an element is a compound. A compound is a mixture of two or more elements, e.g. water.
- **Physical change:** This happens when the appearance of a thing changes, although there has been no chemical change, i.e. water changes to ice when exposed to extreme cold.

Physical processes

This section of the test paper will deal mainly with physics. Children will be expected to have a working knowledge of electricity, forces and motion, light and sound and the Earth and beyond.

What the examiners will be looking for

Your child will be expected to display a basic understanding of electricity and to know how to construct an electrical circuit, using a battery, wires and a bulb in a holder. She should also realise that a circuit may be broken if an object which does not conduct electricity is inserted into the circuit. She should also be able to explain that magnets attract some objects but not others. An understanding of the fact that fuels provide energy is required, and she will also be expected to know that forces can start objects moving and keep them moving. She should have a basic grasp of the sources of sound and light, and demonstrate an understanding of the place of the Earth in the universe.

At Level 4 the average child should understand how to make and operate electrical circuits, the basics of gravity and magnetism, friction, how sound and light travel and how the position of the Sun seems to change over the course of a day.

At Level 5 the emphasis will be on understanding how changes occur. Children will be expected to understand more about the effects of the movement of the Earth round the Sun to produce the seasons and change day to night, be able to change sounds by altering pitch, understand that objects are seen when the light from them enters the eye, and know how to alter the current in a circuit.

Studying physical processes at home

Let your child experience energy at first hand, seeing how the house is heated and lit. Help her to play with toys powered in different ways – by clockwork, elastic bands, etc. Encourage her to take an interest in music and the ways in which sounds are produced on different instruments. In your everyday conversation make sure that she understands the principle of the movement of the Earth around the Sun, and why we get the different seasons and night and day.

Study item: physical processes

- Construct a home-made magnet by stroking any steel object against one of the poles of a magnet. Devise tests to see how powerful the magnet is. Make a number of magnet sculptures. Magnetise many different small objects by stroking them repeatedly along the pole of a strong magnet. The magnetised objects should stick together. Make sculptures from them.

- Experiment with ramps and wheeled toys to test the ways in which the toys can be made to speed up or slow down.
- Make an illustrated list of musical instruments powered by electricity.

Key facts to learn about physical processes

- **Atoms:** Everything is made up of atoms, too small to be seen.
- **Charges:** Inside an atom are two different kinds of electrical charge. These are opposites, like plus and minus signs in mathematics. The charges are called positive and negative.
- **Electrons:** Negative charges are carried by electrons. There are many electrons in an atom.
- **Electricity** When it is disturbed, an electron can leave an atom. It goes to find an atom that has a positive electrical charge. This journey of electrons creates electricity.

SCIENCE TEST PAPER – KEY STAGE 2

Basically, your child will be asked to solve different problems in order to prove that she has grasped most of the scientific concepts described in this chapter. They have been grouped under headings in order for you to see any possible weaknesses in your child's knowledge of the subject.

In each section the questions appear in order of difficulty, starting with the easiest and going on to more difficult ones.

Experimental and investigative science

Time: 30 minutes

Say whether each of the objects below would float or sink if placed in a bucket of water.

SCIENCE TESTS FOR TEN- AND ELEVEN-YEAR-OLDS

1 an iron bar
2 a matchbox
3 a feather
4 a stone
5 What do you think would happen if you put a nail in a bowl of water and left it there for a month?
6 What mixture of substances would cause this to happen to the nail?
7 What change will happen to water if it is boiled in a kettle?
8 What will cause this change?
9 What does the word *vibration* mean?
10 What will happen to the sound caused by beating a drum when the vibrations stop?

Life processes and living things

Time: 40 minutes
Say what each of these parts of a plant does to help the plant grow and stay alive:

1 root
2 stem
3 flower (in most plants)
4 In what way do the roots of a plant prevent the plant for searching for food?
5 Draw a food chain involving at least four different creatures or organisms.
6 What stage is missing from the water cycle given on the next page?

    (a) Water falls to Earth in form of rain.

    (b) Water lies on Earth in rivers, ponds, etc.

    (c) ?

    (d) The vapour rises, cools, forms in clouds and falls to Earth as rain again.

7 Name two ways in which the coat of a polar bear helps it in its environment.

8 Explain the parts played by the teeth and the stomach in the taking in of food.

9 What does food provide us with?

10 Name any two plants whose seeds disperse in different ways. Say how their seeds are dispersed.

11 What does a *gene* do?

12 Name one useful thing which bacteria can do.

What is the function of each of these teeth?

13 incisor

14 molar

15 Air, light and water are all that are needed for what?

Materials and their properties

Time: 40 minutes

Which of these objects are natural and which are man-made?

1 nylon
2 plastic
3 rocks
4 How can you change water to ice?
5 What is an element?
6 What happens to an aspirin tablet when it is placed in water?
7 How does a suspension bridge operate?
8 Explain how a parachute works.
9 What does the word *flexibility* mean?
10 What is a chemical change?
11 You want to take some of the impurities out of some river water. You have a jar of the river water, an empty jar and some blotting paper. What should you do?
12 Name one of the ways in which a sedimentary rock changes over time into a metamorphic rock.
13 Of which three things is water a compound?
14 You have conducted an experiment in which you have put some wire wool in a sealed container of water. You have put some more wire wool in another container of water which is open and not sealed. If you examined both containers after a few days what differences would you expect to see between the two lots of wire? What would account for the difference?

15 Explain the process of *lubrication.*

Physical processes

Time: 40 minutes
Name three things which may be moved by being pulled.

1

2

3

4 Explain how sound is produced from a guitar.

5 When an archer puts an arrow into a bow and pulls back the string of the bow, the power is stored in the bow string. What happens to the power when the bow string is released?

6 Explain how an electrical circuit may be broken.

7 How do we get day and night?

8 What is meant by the *reflection* of light?

9 What is an *atom?*

10 An electron carries a negative charge. When it leaves an atom it goes to find an atom that has a p_____ charge. The journeys of electrons create electricity.

11 What increases the loudness of a sound?

12 We say we are in the Sun's field because it gives two things to the Earth. What are these two things?

13 What is the name given to the gases surrounding the Earth?

14 If you drop a stone and a feather to the ground, which would you expect to reach the ground last? Why?

15 If you looked at your reflection in (*a*) a mirror, (*b*) a window and (*c*) a puddle, you would get a clearer picture in the mirror. Why is this?

Test answers

Experimental and investigative science

1 Sink
2 Float
3 Float
4 Sink
5 It will rust.
6 Mixture of oxygen and metal causes rust.
7 It will turn to steam.
8 Evaporation
9 Shivering, trembling or shaking
10 The sound will stop.

(Total: 10)

Life processes and living things

1 Holds plant in ground, takes in water.
2 Allows water and salts to pass through from roots to rest of plant.
3 In most plants they contain seeds.
4 They anchor it in one place, keeping it stable.
5 Give a mark for any sensible food chain involving four different living things, e.g. flower–insect–bird–human.

6   The heat of the Sun causes the water to evaporate and rise.
7   The heavy fur protects it against the cold, the white colour serves as camouflage against the snow and ice.
8   The teeth chop food into portions and then chew it, thus breaking it down; the stomach digests the food.
9   Energy
10 Give credit for any two sensible answers, e.g. nuts drop to the ground, dandelion seeds are carried by the wind, burrs stick to animals and are carried in that way, etc.
11 Through their genes people pass on certain physical attributes to their children and their children's children.
12 Can be used for making cheese and yoghurt, can be used in making medicines such as antibiotics, can break things up and get rid of waste.
13 Cutting
14 Grinding
15 Growth or life
(Total: 15)

Materials and their properties

1   Man-made
2   Man-made
3   Natural
4   By freezing it or subjecting it to intense cold.
5   A simple substance not mixed up with anything else.
6   It dissolves and changes into a liquid.
7   It hangs or is suspended from steel wires and towers.
8   The open canopy catches the air and is slowed down by the upward pressure.
9   An ability to bend or change shape and return to the original shape without breaking.
10 An entirely new substance is made through the action of one substance on another.
11 Use the blotting paper to filter the water into the empty jar.

12 Give a mark for either pressure or heat.

13 Gases, hydrogen and oxygen.

14 The wire in the water in the open container will become rusty quite quickly because the oxygen in the air has reached it.

15 Oiling or greasing separate parts which work together so that they may move more easily.

(Total: 15)

Physical processes

1,2,3 Give credit for any three sensible answers, e.g. a toy, a tug of war rope, a chest expander, etc.

4 The vibration of the strings when plucked send soundwaves to the ear.

5 The power has been transferred.

6 Insert a non-conductor of electricity into the circuit, or switch it off.

7 The movement of the Earth on its axis around the Sun every 24 hours.

8 Light comes from the glowing gases of the Sun. It bounces off objects and enters our eyes.

9 A group of molecules.

10 Positive

11 The strength or energy with which an object vibrates.

12 Heat and light.

13 The atmosphere

14 The feather, because it would meet with resistance from the air.

15 The surface of the mirror is highly polished and the light rays are reflected in an orderly pattern.

(Total: 15)

Gradings

Give one mark for each correct answer.

Ratings for experimental and investigative science

Marks	Level	Rating
7–10	5	above average
3–7	4	average
0–3	3	below average

Ratings for life processes and living things

Marks	Level	Rating
11–15	5	above average
6–10	4	average
0–5	3	below average

Ratings for materials and their properties

Marks	Level	Rating
11–15	5	above average
6–10	4	average
0–5	3	below average

Ratings for physical processes

Marks	Level	Rating
11–15	5	above average
6–10	4	average
0–5	3	below average

Overall science ratings

Marks	Level	Rating
39–55	5	above average
20–38	4	average
0–19	3 (or below)	below average

Parents talking

❝ *Our child's teacher persuaded us to look after the class hamster during the summer holiday, saying that it would help her revision for the science tests. We woke up one morning and found that the hamster had died. Luckily we managed to get down to a pet shop and replace it before our daughter woke up. She never recognised the difference, and neither did the teacher. We've decided to tell our daughter about it when she's a little older, say 35 or 40.* ❞

❝ *I couldn't understand one of the science projects my child was doing at home, so I went and asked his teacher about it. The man rattled on for about twenty minutes, all of it miles above my head. Then he ended by saying, 'Of course, I'm simplifying it all absurdly.' He could have fooled me!* ❞

Useful books at Key Stage 2

Parents
The Parents' Guide to National Tests Science, HMSO.
Planning Primary Science, R. Richardson, P. Coote and Alan Wood, John Murray.

Children
The Human Body, Steve Parker, Watts.
Back to Basics Science for 9–10-Year-Olds, Godfrey Hall, Letts.
Key Stage 2 National Tests Science, Bob McDuell and Graham Booth, Letts.
How the weather works, Neil Ardley, Dorling Kindersley.
The dictionary of science, Neil Ardley, Dorling Kindersley.

CHAPTER EIGHT

English tests for thirteen- and fourteen-year-olds

Half a dozen children from Year 9 were given some old wrestling magazines and asked to combine to produce a poem on the sport. They decided to base their efforts on the bizarre names of some of the contestants.

Wrestling hall of fame

Tiger Joe, Man Mountain Dean,
Zog the Whip and Hangman Green,
Spiderman, Gorilla Roy,
Yukon Eric, Nature Boy,
Wrestlers all, two falls or one,
Gorgeous George, Atilla Hun,
Savage Schmidt and Caveman Potts,
Dirty Dick, Sweet Daddy Watts
Doctor Death and Moon-Man Dutch,
Zebra Kid, the Spoiler, Clutch,
Chief Big Heart, the Golden Creek,
Sobbing Sid from Cripple Creek,
Youssouf the Bad, Hatchet Man,

ENGLISH TESTS FOR THIRTEEN- AND FOURTEEN-YEAR-OLDS

Judo Jack, Dangerous Dan,
Human Haystack, Tosh Taggo
Top of the bills, long ago.

Class 9

When your child is fourteen he will take two basic papers in English. If he shows exceptional talent he will be given a third test paper to see if he is capable of achieving a very high grading of Level 8 or above.

Paper 1: This will be a test of reading and writing. He will be presented with stories and accounts which he has not seen before and asked to use these as the basis for reading and writing activities – answering questions, stating opinions, engaging in creative writing. Spelling and handwriting will be assessed as an integral part of this test. Your child will be given 15 minutes to read the paper and a further one and a half hours in which to answer the questions.

Paper 2: This will consist of a test based on particular scenes from a play by William Shakespeare. The school will select the play, so that your child will be familiar with it by the time of the test. This paper will occupy one and a quarter hours.

The teacher will also examine course-work done by your child, including speaking and listening, over a period of time and use the results of this work as a part of the final assessment.

Reading

By the time your child reaches Year 9 he will be expected to have read a wide range of literature both in and out of school. He should be familiar with plays, novels, short stories and poetry from different eras, and different kinds of writing – tragedy, farce, comedy, etc.

Your child will be introduced to these different forms of literature at school by his teacher and helped to understand and appreciate them.

142

What the examiners will be looking for

In Paper 1 your child will be given two pieces of writing to read and digest. One of these pieces will probably be an extract from a story or a poem. The other will probably be a piece of non-fiction writing, like an advertisement, a letter, or something similar. There will be questions on the content of the two pieces, the style in which they are written and your child's opinions of various aspects of the examples provided in the test.

In Paper 2 there will be questions based on an extract from a play by William Shakespeare which your child will have been studying at school. He will be given a copy of the extract in a booklet and asked about different aspects of the scene in question. He may be asked about the characters in the scene, the language employed, and the atmosphere developed as the scene progresses.

The examiners will be looking for signs that your child understands and appreciates what he is reading and can express his opinions clearly and in an interesting way, drawing upon a wide range of reading. The very basic standard expected at this secondary stage is that a child shall have read some books published before 1900 and at least one Shakespeare play. To get a good grading, your child's range of fiction and non-fiction reading should be much wider than this.

To receive an average grading of Level 6 a child should be able to understand different levels of meaning in a passage and give his own personal feelings about what he has read, illustrating these with examples from the text.

At Level 7, a child should be able to go into more depth in his analysis of a piece of writing. He should be able to respond to it personally, stating what he likes or dislikes about it. He should be able to refer to examples to support his opinions about the characters, themes and structures. He should also be able to obtain information from various sources and make summaries of this information.

A few gifted children will be allowed to take an extra paper to see if they are capable of reaching Level 8. Children of this ability will be expected to analyse many sorts of writing in depth, depicting their responses clearly and with sensitivity. They should be able to extract different shades of meaning from the texts they read.

Studying the reading tests at home

Revise the points made in Chapter 5, English for ten- and eleven-year-olds. These still apply at this level, only to a more detailed extent.

Liaise with your child's school as closely as possible. Find out which books and plays are being read at school and whether the teacher would like to encourage your child to carry on reading them at home and to discuss them with you.

If the teacher feels that he is doing as much as needs to be done at school with these particular texts, then help your child to read a wide variety of books and magazines at home. It does not matter what this reading matter consists of, the important thing is that he maintains the reading habit.

Try to set aside a little time each week for your child to practise written answers on a piece he has read. This could be an article in a motor-cycle magazine, an interview in a football programme, or whatever. The content does not matter. What is vital is that he begins to practise answering questions on texts in a certain manner.

Study item: responding to a text

When he is answering questions on any piece of writing your child should develop the following techniques:

- read the passage carefully
- work out what points the writer is trying to make
- understand the general sense of the text
- make notes as you read
- answer clearly but briefly – do not waste too much time on any one answer
- select relevant passages from the text to back up or support answers
- check the details of an answer against the text
- be accurate.

In the fiction stories and passages which your child will be tested on there are certain areas in which he should gain practice. In particular he should study *relationships, feelings* and *themes.*

Relationships

Try to get your child interested in the relationships in the stories he reads. Who is the hero or heroine? Who are the friends of the leading character? Who are the enemies? How can you tell? Encourage your child to work out these relationships after he has finished reading a story.

When he has finished a story get him to compile a brief chart to work out how the various characters relate to one another.

Study item: relationships
Name of book: _____
Main character in book: _____

Friends of the main character

1. Name of friend	2. Name of friend	3. Name of friend
_____	_____	_____
How do you know?	How do you know?	How do you know?
_____	_____	_____
_____	_____	_____
_____	_____	_____

Enemies of the main character

1. Name of enemy	2. Name of enemy	3. Name of enemy
_____	_____	_____
How do you know?	How do you know?	How do you know?
_____	_____	_____
_____	_____	_____
_____	_____	_____

Feelings

Help your child to analyse the feelings of characters in stories. From this it should be possible to work out how each character will respond to events and situations.

Study item: relationships

Book:	*Treasure Island*
Event:	Jim Hawkins overhears the crew members plotting to take over ship.
Jim's feelings:	Fear
Causing him to:	Run to his friends and tell them of the plot.
Poem:	*Abou Ben Adhem*
Event:	Abou is told by the angel that his name is not in the list of those who love the Lord.
Abou's feelings:	Sadness
Causing him to:	Think, and tell the angel that he loved his fellow men.

Themes

A theme is the basic idea behind a story, the power which gives a story its thrust and motivation. The theme of *Hamlet* is indecision. The theme of *Dick Whittington* could be perseverance, and so on.

Encourage your child to discuss the themes of the stories he has read. 'Your story is about some children helping a lost dog, so the theme could be *consideration* or *kindness.*'

Writing

After your child has completed the reading tests in Paper 1 he will then be asked to produce a piece of creative writing. He will be given 35–40 minutes in which to do this. There will be a choice of subjects from which to choose. He may be asked to write a story, an article, a letter or something else. Handwriting, spelling and punctuation will all be judged by the examiners.

What the examiners will be looking for

A child of average ability should achieve a pass at Level 5 or Level 6. The standards expected at Level 5 are described in Chapter 5.

At Level 6, the writing produced should hold the interest of the reader and be written with style and confidence, using a varied vocabulary.

To achieve an above average grading of Level 7 the examiners will be looking for an ability to select the right style, with well-drawn characters and ideas which are organised in a coherent and confident manner.

If a child is to be selected to complete additional work to see if he is capable of reaching Level 8, he should be able to write with great confidence, marshalling ideas, events and characters in an interesting manner. Grammar, punctuation and spelling should all be of the highest standards.

Studying writing at home

Encourage your child to write at home in as many different ways as possible, producing answers to reading tests, writing letters, compiling a diary, etc. Check his spelling and punctuation and make sure that his joined handwriting is always clear and legible, no matter how fast he is writing.

Give your child practice under test conditions by giving him a choice of subjects from which to choose one and then ask him to write a finished story or piece of non-fiction writing in 40 minutes.

Study item: writing tips

- Read the choice of subjects carefully before making a choice.
- Spend five or ten minutes making notes.
- Organise your notes in paragraphs, one main idea to each paragraph.
- Make sure that there is a definite beginning, middle and end to your piece of writing.

Encourage your child to select a subject in which he has had some personal experience which he can weave into his piece of writing. The examiners are looking for signs that a child can connect his writing with his world and his experiences. If this is not possible, alert him to the possibility of referring to relevant books that he has read when he writes his story or account.

When you go through your child's written work with him, read it aloud. Make the point that it should always be interesting. The subject-matter and the approach will help here, but equally important is the style of the writing.

Encourage him to use short sentences and to choose his vocabulary carefully, only using long words if he is sure of their meaning and the context in which they are being employed. Vary the beginnings of sentences and paragraphs in order to avoid monotony. Keep paragraphs fairly short. Check spelling whenever there is any doubt. Do not use slang or colloquialisms.

Study item: types of writing

Your child will have to be prepared to produce any kind of writing in the test. The main divisions are:

- **Article:** General description of some common object – school, parents, friends, etc.
- **Occurrence:** Sequence of events – holiday, adventure, journey, etc.
- **Fiction:** Making up a story – you are lost and alone, etc.
- **Place setting:** Describing a place – the old castle.
- **Characterisation:** Describing a person, animal, etc – my pet.
- **Instruction:** Details of how to do something or get somewhere – operating and cleaning a vacuum cleaner.
- **Point of view:** Discussion or debate on a topic – is fishing cruel?
- **Letter:** Addressing different people – friends, strangers, etc.

Give your child practice in writing about these different kinds of topics, remembering in each case to provide a clear beginning, middle and ending.

Grammar and punctuation

As an integral part of your child's written work the examiners will expect to see a firm grasp of grammar and punctuation. No matter how good his creative writing and comprehension skills, he will lose marks if he does not display an adequate technical grasp of language.

What the examiners will be looking for

At Level 4, your child will be expected to know how to use full stops, capital letters and question marks. To achieve Level 5, he should in addition be able to use commas, apostrophes and inverted commas. At Levels 6 and 7 he should be beginning to use semi-colons, brackets, hyphens and dashes.

Studying grammar at home

Your child's teacher will be concentrating on teaching him the correct use of grammar. You can help by checking this in all his work at home. Give him experience in using all forms of grammar and punctuation. Revise the forms introduced in Chapter 6.

A basic form of English usage which it is important that your child masters before taking the tests is *agreement*. This means that the subject of a sentence and the verb or verbs in the same sentence must agree. Lack of understanding of this subject is one of the most common failings in children taking the tests.

Agreement means that when the subject of a sentence is singular or is about one thing, then the verb must also be singular.

ENGLISH TESTS FOR THIRTEEN- AND FOURTEEN-YEAR-OLDS

Study item: agreement

Subject	Verb	
He	jumps	(the subject and verb are both singular)
The cat	yawns	(the subject and verb are both singular)
They	run	(the subject and verb are both plural)
The mice	squeak	(the subject and verb are both plural)

Work with your child going through stories and articles, pointing out the subject and verb and seeing how they agree. Go through his writing activities with him and make sure that the sentences are in agreement.

There are a number of other aspects of language which it is important for your child to understand at this stage. In particular, make sure that he knows how to use the following aspects of language.

Study item: punctuation

- **Commas** are used to separate a list of things in a sentence. We do not put a comma before the word *and* at the end of a list: *apples, pears, cherries and grapes.* Commas are also used when we would take a natural pause in a sentence.
- **Question marks** end sentences which ask questions: *What are you doing now?*
- **Exclamation marks** end sentences in which we have exclaimed or shouted: *Come here! This is ridiculous!*
- **Inverted commas** are placed immediately before and immediately after someone has spoken in direct speech: *"Shall we come in?" asked the girls.*
- **Apostrophes** have many uses. They can be used to show who owns something. A singular noun is followed by an apostrophe and an *s*: *the ship's bell; the town's mayor.*
  A plural noun using an *s* is followed simply by an apostrophe: *the wolves' howls; the classes' books.*
  A plural noun not ending in an *s* is followed by an apostrophe and an *s*: *the children's books; the women's coats.*

HELP YOUR CHILD WITH THE NATIONAL CURRICULUM TESTS

An apostrophe is also used when a letter or a number of letters are left out of a word: **I shall not!** = **I shan't!**; **I will not!** = **I won't!**

Spelling and handwriting

Make sure that your child uses a dictionary to check the spelling of words. The more he reads the better his grasp of spelling should become. He should now be writing in legible joined handwriting.

Give him practice in spelling certain types of words.

Study item: words with similar sounds

Give your child the meanings of each pair of words and ask him to spell both words.

allowed, aloud	paws, pause	ball, bawl
beach, beech	flour, flower	die, dye
plain, plane	crews, cruise	heard, herd
sight, site	scene, seen	stair, stare

Study item: words with the same endings

tough	rough	cough	bough	enough
confine	refine	mine	brine	line
bless	confess	dress	guess	less

Key facts about language

- **Anagrams:** Words formed by rearranging the letters of another word, e.g. *rite* can be rearranged to form *tire*.
- **Antonyms:** Words with opposite meanings, e.g. *big, small*.
- **Cliché:** A hackneyed, overworked expression, e.g. 'It was a game of two halves.'
- **Definite article:** The word *the*.
- **Dialogue:** Conversation between people.
- **Euphemism:** A bland means of expressing something, e.g.

'the dog was put to sleep', instead of 'the dog was killed'.

- **First person:** The use of the word *I*.
- **Gender:** The sex of an object, whether a noun is masculine, e.g. *dog*, or feminine, e.g. *bitch*.
- **Jargon:** Technical words or phrases, e.g. 'he sold a dummy, side-stepped and then scored a try in the corner.'
- **Monologue:** A long, uninterrupted speech by one character.
- **Objective:** A dispassionate, unemotional account of something, not disturbed by emotions.
- **Setting:** The place where a story is set, or takes place.
- **Subjective:** An account strongly influenced by emotions or personal feelings.
- **Syllable:** A single unit of sound in a word, e.g. *big* has one syllable, while *important* has three syllables.

ENGLISH LANGUAGE TEST – KEY STAGE 3

Reading

Time: 90 minutes

Read the following passage carefully and then answer the questions on it.

The Man Who Would Manage

It has been told to me that at nineteenth months of age he wept because his grandmother would not allow him to feed her with a spoon, and that at three and a half he was fished, in an exhausted condition, out of the water butt, whither he had climbed for the purpose of teaching a frog to swim.

HELP YOUR CHILD WITH THE NATIONAL CURRICULUM TESTS

Two years later he permanently injured his left eye, showing the cat how to carry kittens without hurting them, and about the same period was dangerously stung by a bee while conveying it from a flower where, as it seemed to him, it was wasting its time, to one more rich in honey-making properties.

His desire was always to help others. He would spend whole mornings explaining to elderly hens how to hatch eggs, and would give up an afternoon's blackberrying to sit at home and crack nuts for his pet squirrel. Before he was seven he would argue with his mother upon the management of children, and reprove his father for the way he was bringing him up.

As a child nothing could afford him greater delight than 'minding' other children, or them less. He would take upon himself this harassing duty entirely of his own accord, without hope of reward or gratitude. It was immaterial to him whether the other children were older than himself or younger, stronger or weaker, whenever and wherever he found them he set to work to 'mind' them. Once, during a school treat, piteous cries were heard coming from a distant part of the wood, and upon search being made, he was discovered prone upon the ground, with a cousin of his, a boy twice his own weight, sitting upon him and steadily whacking him. Having rescued him, the teacher said:

"Why don't you keep with the little boys? What are you doing along with him?"

"Please, sir," was the answer, "I was minding him."

He would have 'minded' Noah if he had got hold of him.

Jerome K. Jerome

Spend at least ten minutes reading this passage before you attempt to answer any questions.

For the first four questions provide at least three or four sentences when you answer. Include words and phrases from the passage to support all your answers.

1 How would you describe the child in the passage if you were a friend of his wishing to emphasise his good points. In your answer refer to the reasons for his actions and say whether he was successful in what he set out to do.

2 How would you describe the child in the passage if you were someone who had to live with him and suffer from his actions? Refer to at least three people or creatures who had cause to be annoyed by him.

3 What was the child's attitude to other children?

4 Give accounts of at least two things that happened to the child before he was four years old.

5 Who was the Noah referred to in the last sentence?

6 Why would Noah have been a particularly unsuitable person to be 'minded' or managed?

7 In the passage stating that the boy tried to tell hens how to hatch eggs, what word in that passage tells us that the hens were experienced?

8 In the sentence beginning "It was immaterial to him whether the other children ...", what does the word 'immaterial' mean?

9 Why was it a pointless job for the boy to try to mind his cousin?

10 What sentence in the passage explains the whole intention of the boy in life?

11 How do we know that the child was still at school?

12 Read the following part of a sentence from the passage: '... nothing could afford him greater delight than "minding" other children, or them less.' What do the words 'or them less' mean in this sentence?

13 Why do you think the writer gave the story the title 'The Man Who Would Manage'?

14 What does the word 'harassing' mean in the phrase 'this harassing duty'?

15 Name two pets that the child had.

Reading

Time: 60 minutes

Spend at least ten minutes reading this passage before you attempt to answer any of the questions.

The Grant Clan

A clan is a Scottish group of families, originally all descended from one family. One of these clans is the Clan Grant. Its members claim to be descended from Kenneth MacAlpine, King of Scotland in the 9th century.

For centuries the Grants were very powerful in the north-east of Scotland. They supported the uprising led by William Wallace in his effort to gain independence for Scotland in 1297. A year later Edward I of England invaded Scotland and defeated Wallace.

A tartan is a woollen cloth woven with bands of different colours and widths, crossing one another at right angles. It is worn chiefly by Scottish Highlanders. The Grants have their own tartan. Their motto is 'Stand fast'. Their crest or badge shows a mountain in flames.

1 Explain exactly what a clan is.
2 Which particular kind of Scot is usually entitled to wear a tartan?
3 Explain exactly what a tartan is.
4 What is a crest?
5 What is the picture on the crest of the Grants?
6 What is a motto?
7 What is the motto of the Grant clan?
8 Whose uprising did the Grants support?
9 Against which country did this uprising take place?
10 In which year did the uprising take place?
11 What did King Edward I do?
12 In which year did he do this?
13 Who are the members of the Clan Grant descended from?
14 When was this man King of Scotland?
15 In which part of Scotland were the Grants very powerful?
16 What is the main intention of this passage?
17 Do you think that the writer is successful in his intentions? Give reasons for your answer.

Writing

Time: 60 minutes
Read the story **The Man Who Would Manage**

again. Imagine that you are a newspaper reporter and that you were present on the school treat when the child was beaten by his cousin for trying to 'mind' him. Write a newspaper account, describing what happened.

- Interview the child and his cousin.
- Talk to the teacher and other children on the treat.
- Include in your story some of the other incidents you have heard about involving the interfering child.
- Give your story a suitable headline.

Test answers

For those answers bearing a total of five marks give your child credit for the fullness of each answer. Extra marks should always be given if an appropriate passage or sentence is quoted from the text.

The Man Who Would Manage

1 The child was good-hearted and well meaning, 'his desire was always to help others'. He would give up hours of his time trying to help pets. 'He would spend whole mornings explaining to elderly hens how to hatch eggs . . .'. He expected nothing in return, taking on these tasks 'without hope of reward or gratitude'. He was always being misunderstood by those he was trying to help, which accounted for his lack of success.
   (5 marks)

2 The child was an interfering busybody, always putting his nose in where it was not wanted, attempting to teach frogs how to swim, cats how to carry kittens and other things which the creatures could do perfectly well already. He was completely insensitive, not realising how much he infuriated others, until his

ENGLISH TESTS FOR THIRTEEN- AND FOURTEEN-YEAR-OLDS

cousin was reduced to 'sitting upon him and steadily whacking him'. Among those he annoyed were his grandmother, parents, cousin, other children, cat, hen, squirrel, bee, frog.
(5 marks)

3 He was bossy and overbearing, liking nothing better than to look after them, even when they did not want to be looked after. His interference was all embracing. 'It was immaterial to him whether the other children were older than himself or younger, stronger or weaker . . .' As soon as he came across others he 'would set to work to mind them'.
(5 marks)

4 He tried to feed his grandmother with a spoon and he climbed into a water butt to teach a frog how to swim, having to be 'fished, in an exhausted condition, out of the water'.
(5 marks)

5 The Noah referred to in the Bible, who built the ark.
(1 mark)

6 Because Noah was a particularly well-organised, resourceful, efficient and determined person, who would require no help from the child. Anyone who could build and stock the ark was not in the need of assistance.
(5 marks)

7 Elderly **(1 mark)**

8 It did not matter, of no consequence, unimportant **(1 mark)**

9 Because the other boy was bigger and stronger, 'twice his own weight'.
(3 marks)

10 'His desire was always to help others.' **(3 marks)**

11 He went out with the school to the woods, 'on a school treat.'
(2 marks)

12 Nothing could give the other children less delight than to be minded by the child; they did not want to be minded by him.
(3 marks)

13 In this case 'would' means 'wanted to'. The story tells of the

childhood of a man who wanted always to be in charge and to manage others.
(3 marks)

14 Difficult, onerous, unpleasant, responsible, troublesome, etc.
(1 mark)

15 Cat (or kittens), squirrel **(2 marks)**

(Total: 45 marks)

The Grant Clan

Give one mark for each of the first 15 answers.

1 A group of Scottish families, originally all descended from one family.

2 Highlander

3 A woollen cloth woven with bands of different colours and widths, crossing one another at right angles.

4 A badge.

5 A mountain in flames.

6 A slogan, a few words describing a principle or intention.

7 'Stand fast'

8 William Wallace

9 England

10 1297

11 Invaded Scotland and defeated Wallace

12 1298

13 Kenneth MacAlpine, King of Scotland

14 9th century

15 North-east

16 To give a brief description of the Grant Clan, giving a short account of where it came from – 'the north east'; something of its history – 'supported the uprising led by William Wallace'; its tartan; its motto – 'Stand fast'; and its crest – 'a mountain in flames'. **(5 marks)**

17 Give credit for any well-reasoned answer which backs up its

opinions with quotations from the passage. It does not matter whether your child likes or dislikes the piece, as long as he can substantiate his views. **(5 marks)**
(Total: 25 marks)

Writing

If you wish to attempt to assess your child's creative writing exercise, the following marks scheme out of 40 may be of use.

Contents	Range of marks
An article with only a shaky resemblance to the facts of the story. Many important points are left out, and the descriptions of the protagonists are poor. The headline is dull and does not highlight the main event. Grammar, spelling and handwriting all very poor.	0–8
An article which manages to include some description of what happened in the wood and who the main protagonistswere. The headline does not have much connection with the facts. Grammar, spelling and handwriting all poor.	9–13
An article containing some details of what happened, with a headline which bears some resemblance to what happened in the wood. The progression of the story is weak and there is little reference to the others present in the wood. Grammar, handwriting and spelling all patchy.	14–19

A reasonably well-presented article with a headline bearing some resemblance to the incident. The description of what happened is fairly accurate and there is some mention of the others present in the wood. Grammar, handwriting and spelling are all fair.	20–25
A sensible article containing most of the relevant points, including interviews with the two main protagonists. The headline is relevant. Grammar, spelling and handwriting are all of an acceptable standard.	26–33
An interesting article with a short, relevant, arresting headline. The details of the scuffle are well presented. There are sensible and interesting interviews with the two protagonists, while the views of others present in the wood are represented. Details of earlier events in the child's life are referred to. Handwriting, grammar and spelling are all of a good standard.	34–40

Gradings

Ratings for reading comprehension

Marks	Level	Rating
55–70	7	above average
40–54	6	average
20–39	5	average
0–19	4	below average

ENGLISH TESTS FOR THIRTEEN- AND FOURTEEN-YEAR-OLDS

Ratings for creative writing

Marks	Level	Rating
34–40	7	above average
26–33	6	average
20–25	5	average
0–19	4	below average

Overall English ratings

Marks	Level	Rating
90–110	7	above average
66–89	6	average
40–65	5	average
0–39	4 (or below)	below average

Parents talking

❝ I tried hard to make my son keep a diary as a part of his preparation for the English tests, but all to no avail. His final remarks on the subject were, "I'm too busy doing things to write about them!" It's a good job Samuel Pepys never took that attitude. ❞

❝ It doesn't exactly fill you with confidence when you ask your son what he's been studying and he answers, "I've did some grammar." ❞

Useful books at Key Stage 3

Parents
The Parents' Guides to National Tests Key Stage 3 English, HMSO.

Children

Revision for English Key Stage 3, Diana Press and Pamela McCamley, John Murray.

Longman Homework Handbooks English Key Stage 3, Alan Gardiner, Longman.

Comprehension to 14, Geoff Barton, OUP.

Discovering Grammar, David Crystal and Geoff Barton, Longman.

Klondyke Kate and Other Non-Fiction Texts, ed. B. Bleiman, S. Broadbent and Michael Simons, English and Media Centre.

CHAPTER NINE

Mathematics tests for thirteen- and fourteen-year-olds

+ *means add*

❨ *increase, amount*
higher, accumulate
sum, total, amass,
substance, greater than, plus, add, quantity,
multitude, rising, soaring, more abundant,
greater, superior,
exceed, growing,
predominate. ❩

Mary, aged twelve

When the time comes for your child to take the mathematics tests at Key Stage 3, her teacher will decide what her capabilities are and then enter her for what he considers to be the correct levels of tests. These tests are known as *tiers*.

Tier 1   Levels 3–5
Tier 2   Levels 4–6
Tier 3   Levels 5–7
Tier 4   Levels 6–8

For each of these tests a child will take two one-hour papers. However, a child taking the Tier 4 papers may also take an extra one-hour paper to see if she is operating consistently at Level 8.

In these papers your child will be given questions covering three areas: *number, shape, space and measures* and *handling data*. There will be about twelve questions on each paper. In each case 50% of the marks will be allocated to the *number* questions and 25% each to *shape, space and measures* and *handling data*. As usual, your child will also be expected to show that she can use and apply mathematics in a number of practical situations.

The relevant tests will be given to all children considered by the teacher to have reached at least Level 4. Those children still considered to be on Level 3 or below will be given a number of mathematical tasks by the teacher, and as a result awarded a level of 1, 2 or 3.

At the age of fourteen an average child should attain Levels 5 or 6. Anyone not quite reaching this standard will be graded at Level 4. An above average child will receive a grading of Level 7. A few children of exceptional ability will reach Level 8.

Using and applying mathematics

At this level your child will be expected to be able to apply mathematics to everyday situations and solve problems by using her skills and knowledge. There will also be an emphasis on *communicating* – using different forms of communication to convey the answers to problems. Children of more advanced abilities will also be asked to show that they can use reasoning in coming to conclusions.

What the examiners will be looking for

To reach Level 6, your child ought to be able to break down quite complex problems into shorter sub-issues, solving these and then going on to others in a logical manner. She will be expected to use diagrams and symbols sensibly.

In order to attain a grading of Level 7 she ought to be able to use a number of skills to solve problems, including the use of such mathematical concepts and ideas as *hypotheses.*

These are ideas or theories which can explain the facts about something. *The weather forecast for next week is that the temperature each day will be below zero degrees. This means that it will be very cold.* She should also be able to generate her own ideas for solving practical problems.

At Level 8, your child will be expected to use a variety of mathematical techniques, adapting them to the problems being considered. She will make increasing use of symbols in order to explain her answers.

Studying the use and application of mathematics at home

There are three main areas which you can work upon with your child at home at this level in order to help her do well in the tests. If she gains confidence and skill in these aspects of the curriculum, all the other parts should fall into place.

1 Using mathematics in everyday situations
2 Using diagrams, symbols and other forms of mathematical communication
3 Practising the use of hypotheses.

Study item: mathematics in everyday situations

- Keep looking for examples of figures, capacity, weight, time, money, length, around you.
- Collect as many timetables as possible – bus, train, airline, etc. Use them to work out routes and times.
- Work out percentages of numbers. Half of the children had apples – 50% of the children had apples. One in 10 of the potatoes was bad – 10% of the potatoes were bad, etc.
- Work out fractions of areas – half-way along the fence, a quarter of the way to town, etc.

- Calculate amounts and then check them – there are about a hundred sweets in that jar.
- Check bills and invoices, work out what a 10% discount for cash would be. Work out the annual cost of electricity from one quarter's bill.
- Check the price of materials in a shop – if one metre costs £2.45, what would three metres cost, and so on.

Study item: communication

Make sure that your child understands the main types of mathematical communication – diagrams, symbols, etc.

- Practise drawing geometrical shapes – rectangles, triangles, cubes.
- Measure angles, using a protractor.
- Draw maps to scale.
- Draw graphs.
- Prepare charts and tables.
- Devise and solve codes.
- Solve puzzles.
- Make up pencil and paper games.

Study item: hypotheses

Spend time helping your child to make general predictions based upon ideas or information she has. Work out ways of testing these hypotheses.

- In an area with high temperatures, strong winds and little rain it is likely that there will be deserts.
- Strong, athletic children will usually be better at games than small, weak children.

Number

The importance of children gaining a firm grasp of the basics of mathematics is shown by the fact that 50% of the marks in the tests are given for this particular part of the subject. At this level a certain amount of *algebra* is included in the curriculum.

What the examiners will be looking for

A child of average ability should reach Levels 5 or 6. At Level 5 she should be capable of multiplying and dividing by whole numbers up to 1000. She should add, subtract, multiply and divide decimals, calculate fractions and percentages, and solve and check the answers to problems.

In order to reach Level 6 she should also be capable of solving equations, using fractions, decimals and percentages and ratios. She should also be able to multiply and divide with confidence and have a basic grasp of algebra.

An above average grading of Level 7 should entail a child being able to multiply and divide mentally, solve problems involving multiplication and division with numbers of any size, use a calculator efficiently, employ symbols and understand the use of proportions.

A few gifted children will be tested to see if they reach the standard of Level 8. To do this they will be expected to solve complicated problems, display a comprehensive knowledge of algebra and interpret a wide variety of graphs.

Studying number at home

You can help your child by giving her practice in those areas which will probably form the basis of most of the mathematical test papers she will take at this stage:

- the four rules (addition, subtraction, division, multiplication)
- prime numbers and negative numbers
- algebra
- equations
- problems.

Make sure that your child can use the four rules confidently. Let her practise adding, subtracting, multiplying and dividing using single digit numbers:

$8 + 3 + 5 =$ $9 - 7 =$ $8 \times 6 =$ $9 \div 3 =$

When your child shows that she can do these sums easily, go on to using tens:

$24 + 32 + 46 =$ $73 - 45 =$ $24 \times 15 =$ $56 \div 14 =$

From this go on to using hundreds and even thousands. Give your child basic practice in these sums at least once a week. If she proves adept at them, vary the procedure by letting her apply the four rules of weight, time, capacity, length, etc.

Give her simple mental arithmetic tests to complete, and make sure that she can handle a calculator with confidence and ability.

Take time to ensure that she can use decimals, adding, subtracting, dividing and multiplying, and that she can perform simple activities with fractions.

There are a number of other elementary number skills and concepts which your child must be able to master. Give her practice at home in coping with them.

Study item: prime numbers

- A prime number is a number which may be divided by only two numbers – itself and one.
- 1 itself is not a prime number.
- The first prime numbers are 2, 3, 5, 7, 11.
- Practise picking out the prime numbers in lines. Which are the prime numbers below?
  4 5 6 7 8 12
- Write down all the prime numbers between 1 and 100.

Study item: negative numbers

- A negative number is a *minus* number, a number below 0.
- We get negative numbers in weather calculations. The temperature may be 12 degrees below zero. We express this as −12 degrees.
- Practise working with negative numbers: The temperature rises from −5 degrees to +6 degrees. How many degrees has it risen? (Answer = 11 degrees).

Study item: algebra

- Sometimes it is easier to solve problems when letters are used in place of numbers. This is using algebra.
- An example is: $x = 1$ $y = 2$ $z = 3$
  $x + y + z = 1 + 2 + 3$
- Sometimes a letter representing a number is placed next to a number – 5a, 6x, 7y, etc.
- This is a short-hand way of saying that the letter should be multiplied by the number.
- To do this you will be told what number the letter represents.
- If $a = 4$, then $5a = 5 \times 4 = 20$
- If $x = 7$, then $6x = 6 \times 7 = 42$
- Practise doing algebraic sums like this:
  if $b = 4$, what do these numbers represent?
  4b   6b   8b   9b   10b   12b   15b

Study item: equations

- An equation is a statement in mathematics which involves using an equals sign ($=$).
- The purpose of an equation is to balance both sides of the equals sign. The same numbers or letters should be added to or taken from each side for them to remain in balance.
- $x = 3$ in this equation
  $4x - 5 = 7$
- Practise doing equations of this sort, but do not tell your child what the letter represents. See if she can work it out for herself:
  $5b + 4 = 19$. What is b?
  (What number multiplied by 5 is 4 less than 19?
  $= 5 \times 3 (= 15) + 4 = 19$, so $b = 3$).

Also give your child the chance to solve problems at home. A problem is a mathematical question. Make sure that your child always reads the problem carefully, so that she is sure what is required of her.

Study item: examples of problems

- If six packets of coffee cost £3, what will one packet cost? (Answer: One packet will cost one-sixth of £3. Divide £3 by 6 = 50p)
- A train travels 60 km in an hour. How long will it take to travel 20 km? (Answer: 20 km is one-third of 60 km, so it will take one-third of the time. A third of an hour = 20 minutes).

Let your child start practising with simple problems like this and gradually work her way up to more difficult ones.

Key facts

• **BODMAS:**	A memory aid for working out the order for tackling problems involving a number of stages, e.g. $4 - 3 + 5 \times (4 - 2)$. The order in which these sums should be worked are Brackets, Of, Division, Multiplication, Addition, Subtraction.
• **Compound interest:**	When interest is built up on top of previous interest, e.g. £10 invested at 10% will reach £11 at the end of the first year. At the end of the second year the sum will rise to £11 plus 10% of £11, and so on.
• **Proportion:**	The comparative relationships between two numbers, e.g. as 4 is to 2, so 8 is to 4.

Shape, space and measures

A child will be expected to understand 2D and 3D shapes, be able to draw angles, measure and estimate, work with lengths, areas and volume.

What the examiners will be looking for

At the average grading of Level 5, your child should also be able to draw angles, understand symmetry and understand the metric measuring system.

To achieve Level 6, still considered an average grading, her understanding of geometrical shapes should be even more extensive and she should be able to find the circumference of circles and be able to solve geometrical problems.

At Level 7, the above average grading, she must also be able to calculate lengths, areas and volumes in different shapes.

At Level 8, an understanding of a number of technical terms will be required, as will the ability to use the right geometrical formula to solve a problem.

Studying shape, space and measures at home

If your child can grasp the meaning of a number of concepts she should be able to acquit herself well in this section of the test. Show her pictures and examples of as many basic shapes as you can. Test her until she can identify them with confidence. These shapes should include *square, triangle, rectangle, sphere, cylinder, pentagon, octagon*.

Some of the most important aspects of shape, space and measures to be studied at this level are:

- co-ordinates
- area
- angles.

Study item: co-ordinates

- A co-ordinate is a point used to show the location of an object.
- Draw a set of intersecting lines on a page. These will form a set of squares. Number the lines from 0 to 5 along the bottom and 0 to 5 up the sides.

- Draw a plan of a room, garden, etc. over the squares. This will mean that each object on the plan will be in one of the squares.
- Provide the co-ordinates for an object on the plan. This is done by counting across to the horizontal line nearest to the object and then counting up to the vertical line nearest to the object. If the horizontal line is 3 and the vertical line is 4, then the co-ordinates are (3, 4).
- Draw a series of plans like this and provide the co-ordinates for all the objects on the plans.

Study item: area

- The area of an object is how much surface it has.
- We can judge the area of a square or rectangle by drawing each one on squared paper and counting the number of squares in each one.
- We can use more accurate measurements of an area by multiplying its length by its width.
- Draw a number of squares and circles. Measure the width and length of each one and multiply them to find the area.

Study item: angles

- An angle is the space between two lines which meet or cross.
- Angles are measured in degrees.
- There are 360 degrees in a full turn, 180 degrees in a half turn and 90 degrees in a quarter turn.
- An angle of 90 degrees is called a right angle.
- Measure a number of angles, using a protractor.

Handling data

Children will be expected to show that they can understand different forms of mathematical communication and present their own findings using a variety of forms.

What the examiners will be looking for

The expectations of the examiners will vary from the ability to handle a computer and draw diagrams at Level 4, through a relatively thorough understanding of probabilities and ways of describing problem-solving experiments at the average levels of 5 and 6, to a much more sophisticated understanding of bias, frequency tables and other forms of data representation at the above average levels of 7 and 8.

Studying data handling at home

Information is sometimes much more easy to understand when it is presented in the forms of graphs, tables and diagrams. In order to reach an average rating in the data collection section of the test, your child should be able to demonstrate an understanding of a number of forms of mathematical communication and the ability to use this understanding.

Some of the most commonly recurring topics in the data tests at Key Stage 3 are *discrete data, continuous data, tally charts, frequency tables* and *pictograms*.

Study item: discrete data

- Discrete data is the name given to a number of separate pieces of information under the same heading. These numbers cannot change.
- An example of this could be the number of children in a family at a given time. There might be no children, or one, or three, etc. These numbers cannot be changed.
- Make a list of examples of discrete data. Add to this list every week.

Study item: continuous data

- Continuous data is the term given to information which cannot be pin-pointed like discrete data.

- An example of this could be the life-span of a battery-powered torch.
- Make a list of examples of continuous data. Add to this list every week.

Data is often presented in the form of a *chart*. A common form of this is a *tally* chart. A tally chart is used to make sense of data. A column is drawn in which the information is put down in order. Instead of using numbers we use notches or straight lines.

Study item: tally chart – children's marks in a test

Mark	Tally
0	11
1	111
2	111
3	1111
4	1111
5	11

The results of tally charts are often used to compile *frequency tables*. A frequency table is used to show how many times an event occurs. A frequency table could be produced from the information on the marks tally chart shown above.

Study item: frequency table – children's marks in a test

Mark	Tally	Frequency
0	11	2
1	111	3
2	111	3
3	1111	4
4	1111	4
5	11	2

Practise drawing up tally charts and constructing frequency tables from these. The tests sometimes ask children to construct different forms of graphs from information provided in frequency tables, so let your child try to do this as well.

MATHEMATICS TESTS FOR THIRTEEN- AND FOURTEEN-YEAR-OLDS

Study item: bar graph – number of vehicles passing house in an hour

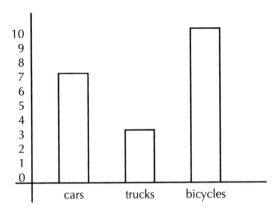

A *pictogram* uses pictures to convey information in an interesting and dramatic fashion. In order to show how many cars are produced each month in a factory, a chart might show a different number of pictures of cars in the column for each month. In this pictogram it would be stated, for example, that each picture of a car represented twenty real cars. Encourage your child to devise and draw her own pictograms in this fashion, providing such information as the number of letters delivered to the house each week.

MATHEMATICS TEST PAPER – KEY STAGE 3

Number

Time: 40 minutes
Add these sums

1	56	2	63	3	74	4	25	5	18
	18		34		78		56		73
	+23		+45		+15		+23		+57

Subtract these sums

6	46	**7**	54	**8**	234	**9**	438	**10**	689
	−35		−26		−167		−369		−458

Multiply these sums

11	56	**12**	45	**13**	78	**14**	135	**15**	238
	× 7		× 9		×12		× 6		× 10

Divide these sums

16 73 ÷ 5   **17** 87 ÷ 4   **18** 234 ÷ 7

19 267 ÷ 15   **20** 4567 ÷ 23

21 What is the value of x in this equation?

$2x = 10$

22 What is the value of y in this equation?

$y - 23 = 13$

23 What is the value of z in this equation?

$14 + z + 3 = 24$

Using mathematics

Time: 20 minutes

1 A caterer has a scale of charges directly proportional to the number of people she is catering for. For a wedding reception for 250 people she charges £850. How much would she charge for a party of 180 people?

2 Two partners agree to invest £54,000 in a business. One partner has more money than the other. They agree to invest the money at a ratio of 2 : 7. How much money does each invest?

3 Work out this calculation by rounding the number off and giving the approximate answer. Show all your working.

16.21 ÷ 3.89 = ?

4 How would you attempt to prove or disprove the hypothesis that tall soldiers are better shots than short soldiers?

5 In a school half of all the girls and a quarter of all the boys have black hair. There are 126 girls and 140 boys in the school. How many children have black hair?

Shape, space and measures

Time: 30 minutes

1 Find the volume of a cuboid 15 metres long, 14 metres broad and 6 metres high.

2 What is the name given to a three-dimensional object in the shape of a tall, round tin?

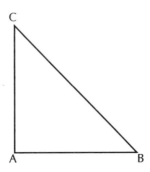

3 Between which two points on this triangle is the hypotenuse?

4 Which letter is nearest to the angle of 90 degrees?

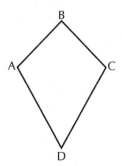

5 Which line is the same length as A-B?
6 Which line is the same length as A-D?
7 Which angle is the same as the one marked by the letter A?
8 Between which two letters does the line of symmetry run?
9 If the formula for finding the volume of a pyramid is $\frac{base\ area\ \times\ height}{3}$ what is the volume of a pyramid with a base area of 10 metres and a height of 12 metres?
10 What is the radius of a circle which has a diameter of 6 cm?
11 How many sides do these shapes have?
quadrilateral   pentagon   hexagon   octagon
12 If the equation for finding the volume of a prism is
area of regular cross section × length of prism
what is the volume of a prism that has a regular cross section of 5 cm and a length of 12 cm?

Handling data

Time: 30 minutes
1 If you were to invest £100 in a bank at

compound interest of 10%, how much would you expect to see in your bank statement at the end of two years?

2 The figures below are out of order. Put them in order and say which one is the median.
70 40 20 30 50

3 What is the range of these figures?
5, 7, 9, 11, 15, 21, 25, 27

How would you interpret these powers:

4 6^3
5 10^2
6 8^3

The crowds attending the first football match of a season, rounded up to the nearest thousand, for a number of years were:

1994	1995	1996	1997
45,000	40,000	38,000	36,000

7 After the opening 1994 game, 15% of the crowd stayed away from the game the following week. How many came to the second game in 1994?

8 After the first game of 1997, the Chairman decided that the club needed a 12% increase in attendance if the club was not to lose money. How many people was he hoping for in the second match of the 1997 season?

9 How many fewer people attended the 1997 game than saw the 1994 match?

10 The average price of admittance for the 1995 game was £12.50. What was the total amount taken? (You may use a calculator to work this out.)

Test answers

Number

1 97	**2** 142	**3** 167	**4** 104	**5** 148	**6** 11		**7** 28
8 67	**9** 69	**10** 231	**11** 392	**12** 405	**13** 936		**14** 810
15 2380		**16** 14 r 3		**17** 21 r 3			**18** 33 r 3
19 17 r 12		**20** 198 r 13		**21** 5	**22** 36	**23** 7	

(Total: 23)

Using mathematics

1 £612

2 £12,000 and £42,000

3 16.21 rounded down = 16, 3.89 rounded up = 4, answer:
 16 ÷ 4= 4

4 Test the shooting ability of the soldiers and draw a scatter graph to see if there is any correlation with height.

5 98

(Total: 5)

Shape, space and measures

1 1260
2 cylinder
3 C-B
4 B
5 B-C
6 C-D
7 C
8 B-D
9 40
10 3
11 4, 5, 6, 8
12 60

(Total: 12)

Handling data

1 £121
2 20, 30, 40, 50, 70; m = 40
3 22
4 $6 \times 6 \times 6 = 216$
5 $10 \times 10 = 100$
6 $8 \times 8 \times 8 = 512$
7 38,250
8 40,320
9 9000
10 £500,000
(Total: 10)

Gradings

Number

Marks	Level	Rating
17–23	7	above average
13–16	6	average
11–15	5	average
0–10	4	below average

Using mathematics

Marks	Level	Rating
5	7	above average
4	6	average
3	5	average
0–2	4	below average

Shape, space and measures

Marks	Level	Rating
9–12	7	above average
7–8	6	average
5–6	5	average
0–4	4	below average

Handling data

Marks	Level	Rating
8–10	7	above average
6–7	6	average
4–5	5	average
0–3	4	below average

Overall mathematics ratings

Marks	Level	Rating
38–50	7	above average
30–37	6	average
20–29	5	average
0–19	4 (or below)	below average

Parents talking

 It didn't matter how hard I tried I couldn't get my husband to help our son at home. Then one day I came home late to find them both engrossed in maths problems. Later on I asked

my husband why he had suddenly taken such an interest. He said our son was having difficulty in understanding negative numbers. My husband had dug out a few of our old bank accounts and pointed out the figures in red. He said our son had cottoned on at once. ❜

❛ *I worked really hard at mathematics to try to keep one step ahead of my daughter, but I found equations really difficult. I went along to an open evening at school and saw the maths teacher and went through the different stages with him. He said that I had really grasped the principle of the thing and would I like to come in once a week and do a little part-time tutoring with small groups. The awful thing was, I don't think he was joking!* ❜

Useful books at Key Stage 3

Parents
Longman Homework Handbooks, Key Stage 3, *Mathematics*, Brian Speed, Addison–Wesley Longman.

Children
Foundation Maths, Anthony Croft and Robert Davison, Longman.
Foundation GCSE Mathematics, A. Ledsham and M. E. Wardle, OUP.
Key Stage 3 National Tests Mathematics, Mark Patmore and Brian Seager, Letts.

CHAPTER TEN

Science tests for thirteen-
and fourteen-year-olds

Injury time
(The old footballer's lament)

1.
I used to be a goer,
A wizard on the ball.
But now I'm old and slower,
And no one cares at all.

2.
My hamstring went at Mansfield,
My tendon at the Dell,
A shoulder cracked at Anfield,
You should have heard me yell!

3.
I broke my nose at Chester,
An ankle turned at Crewe.
I lost three teeth at Leicester
And then we only drew.

4.
My knee-cap cracked at Barrow
A pelvis strain at Hesse,
A shin-bone gash at Carrow.
They'd shoot a horse for less!

Brian and Tim, Year 9

These two boys were asked to make a study of stresses on the human frame. They did it in an unusual way, based on their love of football.

When the time comes for your child to take the science tests in Year 9, his teacher will make a judgement according to the ability he has shown in the subject on a day-to-day basis. As a result of this your child will be entered for one of two tiers. *Tier 1* will be for children considered capable of achieving a grade somewhere between Levels 3 and 6. *Tier 2* will be for children who are thought to be able to attain a standard between Levels 5 and 7. A child entered for the Tier 2 tests may also be entered for an extra paper to see if he is operating at Level 8.

There will be two papers in each of the main tier tests, each one lasting about an hour. The tests will cover all the main areas of science which the children will have been studying – biology, chemistry and physics. They will also be expected to show that they know how to experiment and investigate in a scientific manner.

An average child should be capable of achieving a standard of Level 5 or Level 6. Level 7 is an above average score. A child capable of achieving a Level 8 grading is doing very well indeed. The standards necessary for Level 4 and Level 5 gradings, and suggestions as to how these grades may be prepared for, will be found in Chapter 7.

Experimental and investigative science

Science is essentially a practical subject and your child will be expected to demonstrate that he recognises this and can apply his skill and knowledge to a variety of situations.

What the examiners will be looking for

At Level 6 your child ought to be able to observe and measure with accuracy, and make predictions as to what might happen, based on the knowledge he has acquired and what he can see and sense.

At Level 7 he should be able to pick out the important factors in situations. He should also be able to devise and conduct experiments in order to pick out vital data. He should then be able to present this data in graph form and draw conclusions from it, explaining clearly what has been done.

To be graded at Level 8 he should be able to choose the right strategies in order to obtain information, manipulating scientific instruments with understanding and skill. He should also be able to analyse his own work, pointing out shortcomings and, where necessary, repeating experiments.

Studying investigative and experimental science at home

Help your child to think scientifically. Encourage him to wonder why things which happen in the house actually do happen and to look for the answers to his questions. Devise an investigation plan which may be used as the starting-point for work done at home. Try to complete one plan every two weeks or so.

INVESTIGATION PLAN

1	**Decide**	What are you going to investigate?
2	**Predict**	What do you think will happen as a result of your investigation?
3	**Plan**	Which key factors do you think you will have to cover during your investigation?
4	**Locate**	Will you have to go anywhere in particular to carry out your investigation?
5	**Equipment**	What equipment will you need?
6	**Experiment**	Conduct your experiment, enquiry or investigation.
7	**List**	Make a list of the important points which you discover during your investigation.
8	**Repeat**	Repeat the investigation, but this time leave out one of the important factors. Does this make a difference to the results?

SCIENCE TESTS FOR THIRTEEN- AND FOURTEEN-YEAR-OLDS

9	**Measure**	Measure the results of the original experiment and the repeated, altered one. Compare the results.
10	**Record**	Write down the results and measurements.
11	**Present**	Present the results and measurements in the most suitable way.
12	**Consider**	Consider the results of the investigation. Can you discover a general pattern which will explain these results?
13	**Judge**	Do the results support your original prediction? Could your investigation have been improved in any way?

Study item: scientific investigations and experiments

- Collect seeds and decide how they are dispersed.
- Collect different pieces of cloth. Devise tests to see which ones (a) are most water-resistant, (b) are least likely to stretch, (c) can be cleaned most effectively.
- Decide which everyday appliances turn electricity into sound.
- Work out a balanced diet which a vegetarian could adopt.
- How can you show that the length of your shadow depends upon the position of the Sun in the sky?

It will also help your child if he learns the meanings of a few scientific words and phrases which are sometimes used in the test papers.

Key facts to learn

- **Bacteria:** Tiny organisms which may cause decay.
- **Classification:** Sorting information into groups.
- **Diffusion:** Movement of particles so that instead of being tightly packed they are now less concentrated.

- **Element:** A pure substance which cannot be split up into anything simpler by chemical reactions.
- **Carnivore:** Meat eater.
- **Herbivore:** Plant eater.
- **Invertebrate:** Animal without backbone.
- **Reaction:** What happens when something is added to or taken from a substance.
- **Vertebrate:** Animal with backbone.
- **Volatile:** Liquid which turns easily into vapour.

Life processes and living things

This section covers biology, the study of humans and plants. It includes the study of cells, life cycles, growing and classification.

What the examiners will be looking for

The requirements for Levels 4 and 5 will be found in Chapter 7. At Level 6 your child will be expected to have a basic knowledge of living things and their life processes. He should understand what cells are and be aware of some of the causes of differences between living things. He should also be aware of the effect of their environments upon living things.

At Level 7 your child should be able to compare different life processes, display a knowledge of cell structures and examine and explain the differences between individuals.

To be graded at Level 8, your child should be capable of predicting and explaining changes in biological systems. He should also be able to understand ecosystems and demonstrate an extensive knowledge and understanding of life processes and living things.

Studying life and living processes at home

Revise your child's knowledge of plants and animals. Help him to understand that living things may be placed in different groups and that they are adapted to survive in their environment, but that outside influences on an ecosystem may change it.

Study item: life and living processes

- Make a list of creatures which seem particularly well adapted to their environments. Say why this is so.
- Make two lists, one of creatures which reproduce by laying eggs and another of those who give birth to live babies.
- Make a list of the invertebrate creatures you can see in your house and garden.
- Make a list of all the different kinds of pollution that you know. Say how each one is harmful and who or what it harms.
- Find out the difference between warm-blooded and cold-blooded creatures and give examples of each sort.

Key facts to learn about living things

- **Food-chain:** Links between eaters and eaten. A cow eats grass and in turn is eaten by humans. A small fish eats sea insects, is eaten by a larger fish, which is eaten by a small bird, which is eaten by a larger bird.
- **Food-web:** When food chains become inter-connected they are known as a food-web.
- **Germinate:** A seed begins to grow.
- **Habitat:** Part of an environment, where creatures live in a community, like a field or hedge.

Materials and their properties

In this section children will continue to develop their knowledge of chemistry. Different materials and their properties will be examined. The ways in which different changes take place will be considered.

What the examiners will be looking for

The skills and knowledge expected for gradings at Levels 4 and 5 will be found in Chapter 7. To reach Level 6 children should be able to describe physical and chemical changes and how new materials can be made. They should recognise that matter is made up of particles. They should be capable of describing the differences between the arrangement and movement of particles in solids, liquids and gases. They should recognise similarities between some chemical reactions, such as acids on metals, or a variety of substances with oxygen.

At Level 7, your child should have a good knowledge of elements, mixtures and compounds. He should also understand how some substances react to one another and why they do this.

To attain Level 8 your child should be able to understand and use chemical formulae and recognise and describe patterns in chemical changes.

Studying materials and their properties at home

Study item: materials

- Make a collection of materials used in the building of a house – bricks, pipes, tiles, etc. Sort them according to their properties. Why was each material selected for its particular function?
- Make mixtures of two different materials – sand and sugar, etc. Work out ways of separating these materials again – filtering, evaporation, etc.
- Make mixtures of different soft drinks until you have developed an attractive taste. Think of a name for your new drink and design a label for it.
- Mix dough to make bread. Experiment with different sized portions of dough and note the different lengths of time it needs to be baked. Discuss the scientific aspects of what you have done. Perform similar experiments with making toast,

varying the thickness of the bread and the length of time it is toasted.
• Make a list of the physical changes and the chemical changes which may occur in the weathering of rocks.

Key facts to learn about materials and their properties

• **Element:** A pure substance which cannot be split into anything simpler.
• **Mixture:** Elements can be mixed together to form mixtures.
• **Compound:** Some mixtures of elements react upon one another to form compounds.
• **Formulae:** A formula is a general law, expressed briefly by a group of letters, numbers or symbols. For example, water is a compound of the elements hydrogen and oxygen. The formula for this is H_2O.
• **Solubility:** When something is dissolved in water it is said to be soluble. There will come a time when no more will dissolve. This stage is known as a saturated solution.
• **Weathering:** The impact of weather on rocks and buildings and other materials is known as weathering. Objects are broken down by the effects of wind, rain, cold, etc.

Physical processes

Your child will be expected to have a good grasp of the basics of physics, including how forces, sound and electricity, and magnetism may be harnessed for our everyday needs, the position of the Earth in the solar system, and sources of energy.

What the examiners will be looking for

The standards expected at Levels 4 and 5 are described in Chapter 7. To reach Level 6, your child will be expected to show that he is capable of understanding abstract ideas based on scientific activities undertaken, as well as demonstrating a grasp of the principles of electricity and magnetism. He should also be able to discuss the planetary system.

At Level 7 your child will be expected to understand materials and the particles of which they are composed, explain differences between elements and compounds, to perform calculations and to use abstract ideas in order to explain certain physical processes like vibration and energy transfers.

At Level 8 your child will be expected to understand the passage of sound waves, interpret graphs, obtain data and explain patterns.

Studying physical processes at home

Study examples of hot and cold things and how they change from one to the other, experiment with sound and light, and look at different forms of forces.

Study item: physical processes

- Experiment with forces by making a number of parachutes of different sizes and with different weights attached. How can the rate of descent be curtailed or accelerated? What scientific principles are involved?
- See how sunlight may appear white although it consists of different colours. Construct a colour wheel, using the colours of the spectrum – red, orange, yellow, green, blue, indigo, violet. Turn the wheel into a spinning top by sticking the stump of a pencil through the centre. Revolve the wheel at different speeds until they merge to give the effect of being white.

SCIENCE TESTS FOR THIRTEEN- AND FOURTEEN-YEAR-OLDS

- Show how force can alter the shape, speed and direction of an object by striking a soft ball a number of times with a hard bat. Record your findings.
- Show how a lever works by constructing one in the shape of a model see-saw. A bar is placed across a pivot. A force applied to one end of the lever starts a movement. Experiment with balances on each side of the see-saw. How much force is needed to move different objects?

Key facts to learn about physical processes

- **Atom:** The smallest part of an element that can exist which possesses all the properties of the element in question.
- **Charges:** These exert forces upon each other. Like charges attract or draw near; unlike charges repel, or drive away.
- **Conductor:** Allows electricity or heat to pass through it.
- **Gravity:** The force which pulls everything to the centre of the Earth.
- **Refraction:** The process of light changing direction as it passes from one material to another.
- **Voltage:** A measure of energy supplied to make an electrical current flow.

SCIENCE TEST PAPER – KEY STAGE 3

Experimental and investigative science

1 If you have boiled some water in a saucepan with a lid on it, some of it will change to steam. What will have collected on the inside of the saucepan lid when you take it off? What will this change back to when the water in the saucepan cools again?

2 In the early days of gold mining, prospectors

would take sieves to streams where there might be gold. Why would they do that?

3 If you tied a heavy stone to a piece of string and placed it in a bucket, how would the stone feel as you pulled it up through the water? Why would it feel like this?

4 Sometimes a piercing noise can shatter a thin wine glass into pieces. Why does this happen?

5 Why do plants of the same species vary in size when they are picked in different places?

6 Bacteria cannot grow easily in salt. How could you use this knowledge in a practical way?

7 Which ingredient could you leave out of dough if you did not want a loaf to rise?

8 Give any one variable which might affect the growth of a plant.

9 Why does a doctor us a stethoscope to listen to the beating of a patient's heart?

10 If you leave a battery-operated torch switched on long enough eventually it will go out. Why is this? Be specific.

Life processes and living things

1 A food cycle shows how living things are eaten by other living things. Green plants are eaten by many different creatures, but most plants do not eat creatures themselves. Why is this?

2 How does the plant called the Venus flytrap differ from most other plants in its method of obtaining food?

3 What do you think there is about the environment that makes the Venus flytrap obtain its food in this manner?

4 How do some small creatures benefit the soil when they eat the dead bodies of animals?

5 When the single-celled creature called the *amoeba* floats through water and finds a particle of food it will change its body shape. Why do you think it does this?

6 Fish use their gills to take in oxygen and get rid of another gas into the water. What is the gas being breathed out called?

7 What is the name given to the collection of bones which protect the lungs in the human body?

8 What is the name given to the system by which blood goes round the body?

9 Many animals can adjust the temperature of their blood, so that it remains at the same level, no matter what the weather or their environment. The desert iguana lives in deserts. What do you think it does to keep cool?

10 Many desert plants have very short roots, extending just below the surface of the desert. Why do you think this is?

11 *Metamorphosis* means *change*. Describe the four stages of metamorphosis in the life-cycle of a butterfly.

12 What part of the human body consists of cartilage and bone?

13 Which part of the human body controls the sense of balance?

14 Spiders are born with the knowledge of how to spin a web. What is the name given to something that an animal is born knowing how to do?

15 What is the difference between a carnivore and a herbivore?

Materials and their properties

1 What scientific principle are you demonstrating if you strike a match on the side of the box?

2 If a research assistant takes a number of different materials and pours water over each one, what is he probably testing them for?

3 In addition to making an iron gate look more attractive, in what other way would painting it help protect it?

4 The enzyme *amylase* is secreted in saliva. It reacts on large starch molecules and breaks them down into smaller glucose molecules. What is the name given to a substance like this which alters the rate of a chemical reaction without being used up?

5 If we see water being contained in jars of different shapes, what does that remind us about water?

6 What are filtering and evaporation both examples of?

7 If you use the same toaster and toast one piece of bread for two minutes, one for four minutes and one for eight minutes, how would each piece of toast differ?

8 Fill in the two spaces: H_2O is a f_____ for w_____.

9 What is a *synthetic* material. Give two examples.

10 What is the main property of glass that makes it suitable for windows?

11 Why is combustion a useful way of changing wood?

12 How could weathering change a mountain into a hill over a long period of time?

13 Sandy soil has large grains with large holes between them, which allow water to drain away quickly. Clay soil has small grains with small holes between them, which retain water. If you were laying a cricket pitch which sort of soil would you prefer for it? Say why.

14 Plastic is made chemically from oil or coal. It starts as a soft, pliable material and then hardens. Why does this make it popular with manufacturers?

15 A primitive man wanted to obtain salt from sea water, so he filled a shallow hole in a rock with sea water and waited for something to happen to
give him the salt. What was he waiting for?

Physical processes

1 What is a force?

2 How can you increase the speed of a ball when you throw it?

3 Give an example of a non-contact force.

4 A pressure point occurs when a lot of force is concentrated into a very small area. Where would the pressure point of a nail be?

5 If you use a narrow wood plank as a bridge across a long river bed, what would be a sensible way to strengthen the bridge?

6 If you wanted to test the length to which a spring will stretch you could experiment by hanging different weights on the end, until the

spring is fully extended. Hook's Law states that *extension is proportional to the load*. What does this mean?

7   The tilt or angle of the Earth's axis affects its exposure to the Sun at different times. This gives us seasons. What would happen if there was no tilt and the North Pole faced the Sun permanently?

8   What is *oxidisation*?

9   Give an example of heat conduction.

10   What is the name given to the curved path upon which the Earth travels round the Sun. It begins with the letter e_____.

11   What does the gravitational pull of the Moon on the oceans cause?

12   A man cannot lift a heavy barrel on to a stage, but he can roll the same barrel up an inclined plane on to the stage? Why is this?

13   Why would a driver put anti-freeze into the cooling system of his car in winter? Be specific.

14   Draw a picture showing where the nucleus of an atom would be.

15   Give an example of how a reaction may be increased if the temperature is raised.

Test answers

Investigative and experimental science

1 Water vapour, water
2 They would filter the water through the sieve and inspect the solids left in the sieve, to see if there was any gold among them.
3 It would feel light because the water would support the stone.
4 Heavy vibrations cause sound waves powerful enough to break the glass.
5 It depends on the qualities affecting growth – soil, sunshine, rainfall, temperature etc.
6 Give credit for any sensible answer, like packing food in salt in order to preserve it.
7 Yeast
8 Give one mark for any one of: light, water, soil.
9 It makes the heart-beats sound louder.
10 Eventually the supply of electricity stored in the battery will run out.
(Total: 10)

Life processes and living things

1 They produce or make their own food.
2 It traps and digests insects
3 They exist in areas where the soil is too poor to provide sufficient food for plants.
4 They break down the dead bodies into simple substances that are returned to the earth.
5 It surrounds the food particle with part of its body and then absorbs and digests it.
6 Carbon dioxide
7 Ribs or rib-cage
8 Circulation of the blood, or circulation
9 Looks for rocks and other shady places.

10 So that they can soak up any rain that falls.
11 Egg–caterpillar–pupa–butterfly.
12 Skeleton
13 Inner ear
14 Instinct
15 A carnivore is a meat eater, a herbivore is a plant eater.
(Total: 15)

Materials and their properties

1 Chemical change
2 How waterproof each one is (accept solubility).
3 Help prevent rusting
4 Catalyst
5 It has no shape of its own.
6 Separation or separating
7 The first might be slightly browned, the second more deeply browned, the third heavily browned or burnt.
8 Formula, water
9 A man-made material. Give credit for any reasonable examples like nylon or rayon.
10 It is transparent.
11 It means burning and so makes wood useful for fires.
12 Wear away at its peak or summit
13 Sandy soil; it would drain better and stand a better chance of not getting waterlogged.
14 It is easily made into different shapes when soft, and stays in those shapes when hard.
15 The Sun to evaporate the water and leave the salt.
(Total: 15)

Physical processes

1 Give credit for any sensible answer like pushing and pulling.
2 Increase the amount of force or power you put into the throw.
3 Give credit for any sensible answer like gravity, electricity or magnetism.

4 The point

5 Reinforce it with pillars from below.

6 The heavier the load the farther some materials will extend.

7 It would become very hot all the year round, and the ice would melt.

8 When a substance gains oxygen or loses hydrogen.

9 Give credit for any sensible answer like placing the prongs of a fork in hot water to see if the handle becomes warm.

10 Ellipse

11 Tides

12 He lessens the effect of gravity.

13 It lowers the melting point of the water.

14 It should be in the centre.

15 Give credit for any sensible answer like ice melting.

(Total: 15)

Gradings

Give one mark for each correct answer

Ratings for experimental and investigative science

Marks	Level	Rating
8–10	7	above average
6–7	6	average
4–5	5	average
0–3	4	below average

Ratings for life processes and living things

Marks	Level	Rating
12–15	7	above average
9–11	6	average
6–8	5	average
0–5	4	below average

Ratings for materials and their properties

Marks	Level	Rating
12–15	7	above average
9–11	6	average
6–8	5	average
0–5	4	below average

Ratings for physical processes

Marks	Level	Rating
12–15	7	above average
9–11	6	average
6–8	5	average
0–5	4	below average

Overall science ratings

Marks	Level	Rating
42–55	7	above average
31–41	6	average
21–30	5	average
0–20	4 or below	below average

Useful books at Key Stage 3

Parents

Physics Matters, Nick England, Hodder and Stoughton.

Children

Revision for Science Key Stage 3, Joe Boyd and Walter Whitelaw, John Murray.

Study Guide Key Stage 3 Science, Bob McDuell and Graham Booth, Letts.

How Green are You?, David Bellamy, Francis Lincoln.

The Living World: Biology Today, Donald Silver, Kingfisher.

Index